MW00570858

FROM GRANDMA WITH LOVE

Ann Tuites

FROM GRANDMA WITH LOVE

Ann Tuites

STARBURST PUBLISHERS

P.O. Box 4123, Lancaster, Pennsylvania 17604

To schedule Author appearances write:
Author Appearances, Starburst Promotions, P.O. Box 4123
Lancaster, Pennsylvania 17604 or call (717) 293-0939

Credits:
Illustrations by Emilie Snyder

We, The Publisher and Author, declare that to the best of our knowledge all material (quoted or not) contained herein is accurate, and we shall not be held liable for the same.

FROM GRANDMA WITH LOVE

First Printing, 1995

ISBN: 0-914984-61-6
Library of Congress Catalog Number 94-66618
Printed in the United States of America

To
Don,
Donna, Jim, Barb, Tom,
Jeff, Jess, Katharine, Rob,
Kevin, Michael and *Wes*
who make my life
a beautiful journey.

Contents

Part 1

Why I've Written This Book

My Nana

When I was about 10 we moved to a new house. I loved our little old one. It had all kinds of secret closets, a little porch, nooks and crannies, a big apple tree to climb and a fireplace in the living room from ceiling to floor. I didn't want to move. "We have to," said my father, "because Nana is coming to live with us." (I could tell my mother wasn't too happy with the new arrangement. As I lay in my bed at night, I could hear them arguing, 'til the wee hours.) But Nana did move in with us.

The huge old house was kind of creepy, and what happened there really confused me.

Nana was very angry. She didn't want to be there. The family took away her car. I learned many years later that it was because she had tickets for speeding and couldn't see well enough to drive. Nana would sit in her room and pound on the arms of her chair and talk to herself. She would dress herself backwards and wouldn't want me to help her turn her clothes right side out. At night she would roam around the house. I'd awaken to find her standing in my room. Although I wasn't afraid, it startled me. I knew Nana wasn't happy, but she really embarrassed me.

As time went by, Nana would wander down the street and I'd have to go find her and bring her home. She would talk to my friends about people she knew in her childhood. When I was about 14, I brought a boy home to listen to records. Nana came in and said, "I think it's so nice you two are getting married. I hope you'll be very happy." I wanted to crawl under the rug. My parents must have been embarrassed, too, because they never talked about it. I don't think they understood, either. (People didn't in those days.)

One day I was told, "Nana's gone to stay at the state hospital." Now, I won't have to worry about my friends' giggles or funny looks anymore. But my dad was not happy. If I went downstairs at night I would find my dad with tears in his eyes, sitting in the kitchen drinking a glass of warm milk. He'd say it might help him sleep. Still wondering what all this was about, I vowed that this would never happen to anyone I loved.

Why I've Written This Book

I decided to write something to leave to my children. I have often wished that my mother had written more so I could have felt closer to her as I read her words.

After having some "close calls" and realizing the precious brevity of this earthly life that has been given me, there's an air of urgency surrounding me that says I must pass down to my family the only true legacy I value—my loving thoughts. After two years, I still want to hold Mother in my arms and tell her I love her and that I'm sorry that she had to be in a strange place, frightened, lonely and sick.

I began to write in order to tell others, as well as my children, how I feel. I know I can't represent every other aging person. We all behave differently, but we all have similar feelings about growing old.

I realize now that my children will come to a time in their lives when they will have raised their families, done the very best they could, and are ready for some years in which to relax. The next stage comes abruptly, without warning. We, their parents, may then be at a time when we are unable to care for ourselves. Life has come full circle, and now they are the "sandwiched generation." As I look back, I see this stage as a God-given gift. It was a heavy new responsibility, but not without deep satisfaction and fulfillment for me. There were also things that I would change if I had it to do over.

So, what I am saying is that as I write this book I find my purpose changing. It started out almost as a diary of daily events. Then, gradually it changed to an exploration of "Who am I?" From there it went to questions like, "What is life? What is death? and How do I find peace?" At present, it is sharing the things I contemplate with God each day. My goal has gone from seeking notoriety—a best seller, money, to writing about living, being, observing life, and growing in spirit and wisdom. Most of all, it is to write about all the exciting, beautiful thoughts given to me as I experience the privilege of living each day. It is looking at each day as a page in the book of lessons God hands me with love.

The Dilemma

In the summer of 1983 my parents, who were unable to live alone, came to live with us. Coping with the interactions of four generations, often under one roof, was unexplored territory for us. As the years went by, four grandchildren were added to our family, giving many opportunities to practice our principles of encouragement.

Long ago, when the older members of a family became unable to function as well as they had in the past, it was accepted that they had given their talents, strength and skills to raise the family and were now due a much deserved rest. They would still be given jobs that they could do, and would be consulted as respected elders who were wise from years of experience.

The second half of the 20th Century brought a new era, and with it, distinct change. Those of us born during the depression years were taught that to be of value we must be self-reliant, self-sufficient and independent. Instead of stressing family and community, we were told to stand on our own two feet and not be indebted to anyone. We were determined to never get into a situation again where we were "poor" or in need of anyone. As a result, money became our god. We believed that if we had enough money we could solve anything. We believed that the more we could accumulate the less we would have to worry about. We thought that the greatest success we could achieve would be in not having to work and doing anything we desired. Somewhere along the way we forgot the Golden Rule—loving our neighbor as ourselves, or "it is better to give than to receive." The ultimate goal was accumulation of goods and wealth.

Much of the literature we read today says that we must find a way to acquire money to build institutions, so that our elderly will be "taken care of." We justify this because we believe that we can't do it, or, we don't want to do it because we believe it's too difficult.

We do not think of the human being, full of emotions such as love, fear, anger, bewilderment, who suddenly becomes a pawn to be moved to a place where they will be the least "trouble." As a result, most of our seniors find themselves in a situation where they are with strangers, with no opportunity to be a contributing member of society. They experience few interactions involving closeness and love, except for an occasional caring "aide."

As they adjust to the regime of these institutions, the elderly gradually lose more and more of their skills for living. To avoid the disapproval of the staff, they learn to be quiet, obey, and not "rock the boat."

Retirement homes and nursing homes are not the answer. Only when our seniors choose, or become physically or mentally incapacitated to the point where they need skilled nursing care, should we consider uprooting them. Even then, additional skilled care in the home should be the first consideration. Putting a loved one in an institution is signing a sentence of slow deterioration, and finally, an unhappy end to a usually active and productive life.

Many books written today say you must find alternative living arrangements so that you can "save yourself." It doesn't work this way. Visit any support group for caregivers of the elderly and listen to the tragic stories shared by those who are torn by the "no win" situation of caring for their loved ones. If they can figure out a way to pay the costs leveled by honest, adequate health care units, they soon find that their loved one is finding it almost impossible to adjust to the shock of believing they are abandoned in an unfamiliar, frightening, impersonal room where everyone is saying, "This is your home now."

Why are things so different now? Why, as candidates for the label "senior citizen," are we facing years, possibly decades, of our lives in which we feel purposeless, at best—a fifth wheel, at worst—a burden. Looking back on our life, most of us feel that we reached a goal of belonging and coping. But as our bodies and minds began to lose some of their strength and agility, with this came a loss of confidence. With this loss of confidence came a loss of self-esteem and discouragement.

In the past, the older generation was delighted if they lived long enough to be able to experience the birth of a grandchild. Today, great-grandchildren are a common event. Television programs announce, daily, the names of people who have "achieved" the 100 year mark. The medical profession strives to extend life expectancy. As often happens today, modern science has created a monster without first working out how it will tame it. Extended life expectancy is like holding the proverbial "tiger by the tail." Machines can keep us alive, drugs can keep us comfortable, and signed forms can avoid malpractice suits. But how can we insure a quality of life that might be looked upon as desirable?

To me, the way is clear. There is an alternative. Keeping the family together as long as possible makes sense. Keeping it together in an atmosphere of tension, fear and anger, doesn't. We cannot go on as we have, with our seniors feeling that they are useless burdens, and our caregivers becoming more and more bitter, guilty, hurt and hopeless. There is a way to live together in the same house in an atmosphere of harmony and peace.

There usually comes a time when we are no longer able to care for the elderly. But having them live in an institution, no matter how efficiently it is run, should be the last resort. We owe it to ourselves and our seniors to stop believing that there are only two ways to deal with this huge problem. We're looking at life in an "either-or," "black or white," "right or wrong" manner. We are saying that it has to be either a miserable life for generations who live together, or a frightening lonely life in a home away from family.

It doesn't have to be either of these divergent paths. We can live together in an atmosphere of harmony and peace. We don't have to learn a new psychological method. All we have to do is practice the principles of encouragement, love, and forgiveness. A dear friend and colleague used to say, at least once a day, "First you do and then you become."

Part 2

Grandma's Thoughts

Cherished Moments

I'll sing today
I'll dance
I'll laugh
I'll be with those I love
I'll use money for things I want to give away.

Why?

Each day is precious
No one knows how many she has
I'll talk to loved ones
I'll say what I feel
I'll pray
I'll write
I'll draw
I'll listen
I'll work
I'll be patient
I'll take time.

Whenever I feel angry, fearful or sad I will realize the waste of precious moments and . . . I'll forgive and love.

Reflections Of A Grandma On Her "Self"

Joy is one of the experiences that God has planned for us. What we get out of each day is the result of how we perceive it. Each of us can see something entirely different in the same episode. If we can look at the things that happen to us as lessons to learn on our journey toward peace we will find that we are more optimistic and joyful at the end of each day.

I am joyful because I have four children whom I love and who love me. I believe that my children, their partners and their children, are the most precious things in the world. Each day I rejoice that I found a husband with whom I can communicate, solve problems and live. There is a tie between my family and me that is unique and beautiful, deep and wonderful. I like and love these people as they are. I have unconditional positive regard for them. I accept them with all their assets and also the characteristics that I might not choose for me but love as part of them. Being part of them is most important in my life.

What else would I like you to know about me? I have tried to be honest. I have been, if honesty is the opposite of things like lying, stealing, and cheating. But in other ways I haven't. I often agree outwardly to avoid hurting someone or getting their disapproval. I often wear a mask. I am often so concerned about hiding the "real" me that I don't even know who that is.

I like to do things on the spur of the moment. I sometimes do impulsive things that I later regret. I like to be alone, but I also like to be with the people I care about. I tend to rescue, which is not always good for my loved ones. It fosters dependency and hinders growth. If I feel a great need of anything—another person, a substance, a behavior (like pleasing) to fill any inadequacy, then it is an addiction, not a love relationship. For example, we may expect another person to validate us as being worthwhile. We think of this person as someone who will give us comfort, service or approval—hence, a feeling of self-worth. They may be like the parent we thought we had or always wanted. Instead of relying on our own spiritual growth and God, we lean more and more to this other person. However, we usually find him or her unwilling to fill this role for long.

In the case of a substance, it may be alcohol, food or drugs. We believe that, "If a little makes us feel good, more will fill the void and deaden the pain." The results usually are disastrous.

We may decide that some quality we admire is the answer to our feeling of emptiness. For example, we reason that if we could excel, be perfect, we wouldn't feel so empty. If we look to always being right, successful, comfortable, superior, a workaholic, we discover that we are never quite good enough, and the emptiness persists.

Often, when someone asks me to do something and I say "No," I feel guilty. I feel responsible. I then decide that I must work toward improving my "happiness addiction." To do this I must rid myself of that which I use to fill the void.

I'm concerned about the lack of values in the world. One TV show I saw reported that many Americans think it's OK to lie and break laws and cheat if you don't get caught. I'm concerned about pollution and how we're cutting down our forests and killing our wildlife; that money is the most important thing to most Americans; not just to provide for needs, but to "make lots of money." This is what success means to them.

I love doing anything creative: drawing, painting, dancing, singing, playing recorder or piano, planting flowers. I enjoy activities like swimming, exercise, games, hugging, touching, walking, thinking. I like to laugh and cry and get angry. I don't like to be afraid. I'm not often afraid, except about something bad happening to the children or Don. I don't like being closed into something tight and narrow that I can't get out of. I like music with a strong beat. I like almost all kinds of music, especially romantic selections by Streisand or Tchaikovsky, or happy, funny, peppy and loud ones like Country or Bluegrass.

I believe looks aren't important. I admire a nice face or body, but am not worried that I don't look young anymore. I am a child of God. I'm fine just the way I am, and don't have to measure up to what others think of me. Lately, when I get upset I ask God to please help me get another view of the incident and solve my problem. I do this for loved ones, too. I say, "Thank You, God, for helping me and others," even before I see the answer. I'm learning and growing.

I'm beginning to think that everything that makes me sad has to do with my not being able to keep loved ones happy. I must realize that as a child of God *I* have the right and obligation to be happy. I must learn to say "No," and not accept guilt or project guilt to another person. No one is to blame for what happens. God is in control of my life. To advance one step I must solve a problem with love and forgiveness and a change of my perception. I must ask God for help. I will get help from signs, dreams, thoughts that come to me when I ask for help, then I "let go and let God." I think a lot of what I believe has to do with equality. When there is discord I believe that harmony can come only when we treat the other person as an equal—as a brother or sister (who is made in the image of God). If this concept is followed, then I will invite the other person to solve the discord with me. I will share my observations and facts. I will share my feelings. I will be encouraging. I will seek to understand. I will negotiate peace. I will commit myself to actions that may bring harmony.

I do not always do this. Instead, I often get stuck in my emotions and stay there with no action. I often withdraw. I use sarcasm. I use "You always," statements. I punish, compete, compare, bring up the past and use power. But that's okay. I keep trying. All I need is a little "willingness." I must love myself in spite of all my mistakes.

Time For A Change

Did you ever think that life is too short and precious to waste it on being in the wrong job? My husband and I did. It wasn't that we hated our work. It just didn't feel right. Don loved being with people and yet he sat (or stood) eight hours a day in a lab with test tubes and beakers making "Better things for better living.®" I had a fierce urge to help people by educating them about interpersonal relationships. I had reached the "Peter Principle" level of doing school administrative work when I began teaching children how to develop social skills.

You may be saying, "But you can't quit your job, especially if you have a responsibility to your family." That's right! But, there are other options and alternatives to explore. Our (Don's and my) path took a long and sometimes difficult road. While holding down jobs, we completed ten years of volunteering in counseling areas, training in the evenings, classes all day Saturdays and Sundays for eighteen months, then receiving our Masters' Degrees in Counseling. It involved waiting until our four children finished college. It required the patience to gradually build a private practice and a reputation of effective, successful therapy.

I'm not telling you this to prove how wonderful we are. (Some would say that taking a risk of leaving two well-pay-

ing secure professional jobs and striking out into the unknown is stupid.) What I am saying is, "You can do it!" I
believe that each difficult change you and I experience is
another lesson from God.

As Don and I progressed, many of our values changed.
Working with people to change their lives became more important than the amount of the paychecks at the end of the
month. Each new client gave us new insight into our own
lives as they shared their concerns. With the success of ac-
complishing this change came confidence for us to be more
courageous in each new endeavor.

So, I say, "Take the bull by the horns! You can do anything you set your mind to. But never forget to ask the Holy
Spirit for help." If you see life as a parade of disappointments and suffering, it will be that. If you see it as an adven-
ture containing God's lessons, it will be just that!

Will I Ever Run Out Of Love?

There is so much anger in the world today. As I've said
before, I believe the only way to rid our world of anger is to
replace it with love. I used to think if I did this, send back
love whenever I feel an attack, I would be victimized. I
thought people would take advantage of me. That's not
true. Eleanor Roosevelt said, "The only way people can hu-
miliate you is if you allow them to." So, it's all in my head
and how I perceive it. I don't need to protect myself from

being vulnerable. I don't need to defend. My vulnerability is my strength. Giving love to another human being will not deplete me. Each time I send out love God will refill me as a vessel of His love. If I am an instrument of God's love, and my purpose is to do His work, I will be healthy in mind, body and spirit.

Long ago, I asked my dear friend how she could have love for more than one child. She said, "Of course, you always have enough—it just grows and grows." If it's God's love, it's a never-ending pool I can draw from. If I am the one who measures my worth, rather than measuring it by the approval or disapproval of others, what shall be my measuring stick? I succeed and have worth when I accept the lessons God gives me.

When I first began to consciously practice love and forgiveness I would recognize the opportunity after the lesson was sent and say, "Oh, that's what I should have done." Later, as I became more aware, I would see God's challenge during the incident. Then, I sometimes was able to change my actions to love. Each day when my lesson begins, little by little I come to see the opportunity coming and shift gears to an attitude of love.

The more I grow spiritually, the more subtle the signals become. I don't feel such strong emotions. That's good, because I'm not automatically answering my perception of an attack with an attack. It is harder, though, to recognize an opportunity when the signals are less obvious. A signal to give love can be as simple as a tiny feeling of anxiety, a little queasiness in my tummy, or a questioning of my confidence. I hope that's an indication that I am beginning to live in an atmosphere of love. My one goal is for this love to be like a pebble thrown into a pond where the ripples go in ever-enlarging circles, touching more and more brothers and sisters. In doing so, I will make a difference!

How Do The Past And Future Influence Me?

The past is gone. The future is part of God's divine order. I have free will to decide what the future holds. Each happening that presents itself to me will be an opportunity for me to ask, "What are You telling me?" If I ask, the answer will be given. It will be the truth of God, not my perception. The past and future are not important. What I hear at this moment is. If I made mistakes in the past, God has already forgiven me and given me a new day to start the rest of my life. If I fear the future, God will take care of it. All I have to do is ask for guidance in whatever state (situation) I find myself. I must never doubt the truth. If I do, God will forgive that also, seventy-times-seven.

God is using me for his work. I must give the message that He gave me when I was near death. I must give it by thought, word and deed, to as many people as I can touch.

Earlier in my life my mission was to nurture and guide my family. Now, I dedicate myself to express love to everyone

I reach. I believe that, no matter how much I may want my mission to be different, I have reached a new level of learning and teaching. With the help of the Holy Spirit I can spread love in this world. Showing love, forgiving and guiding my family was easy. The next step may be more difficult, but if it's meant to be, God will take care of it. God's Word says He never gives us more than we can bear. When we decide to give or receive love miracles occur. If we let go of fear, we become miracle workers. There is no order of size in miracles. A miracle can be just saying something nice or smiling at someone. When I talk with God I am getting in touch with love. God is love. My aim is to become a channel into which God pours His love. I can then pour it out to everyone I meet. God sent me to give love, not to talk about it. Maybe that's why it's so hard to explain. My responsibility is to be more loving and forgiving. Forgiving is seeing the other person as one made in the image of God. If there is holiness in him, then there is nothing to forgive.

Filling The Hole In My Soul

What part does our faith play in the all-important last act in the play of life? When I was a little girl I knew that God went with me everywhere. I could talk to Him and He would be there and tell me what to do. It was not like a voice booming out of the clouds but more like *Jimminy Cricket* sitting invisibly on my shoulder and whispering in my ear. I knew what was right and wrong, and that God would guide me and forgive me if I chose a mistaken path.

As the years went by, and as I was bombarded on all sides to be independent, I began to believe that God had left me. I didn't consult Him very often, and when I did, I felt that He was no longer close to me. It never occurred to me that just the opposite was true. My priorities had put God at the bottom of my list. My faith had grown rusty from lack of use, from not getting in touch with Him each day, sometimes many times a day. I was the one who thought God had abandoned me when actually I had chosen to see myself separate from Him. It took many years of loneliness, emptiness and crises to make me realize that He, the Holy Spirit within me, had never left and was eager to welcome me back, whenever I was ready. As I look back I know that whenever things got tough, and my ego (self) couldn't seem to handle life, God gave me small nudges to tell me He was there. Those times I'd say, "See, I do all these things the way I should, and yet God doesn't reward me." I didn't realize that each problem, each new crisis, was a lesson that God was giving me so I could grow in faith.

Early in marriage and motherhood I would awaken to find that during my sleep a dream had been given to me. I'd get the answer to what I believed was an overwhelming problem.

Once in a Christmas Eve service I was in the midst of a panic attack, wondering if I would be able to get through the next twenty-four hours with my parents, husband and four children all expecting me (I thought) to be a *Super Mom*. At that moment I thought I had to bolt and run from the front pew when a miraculous sense of peace enveloped me and I knew I was being held in the arms of God. Wouldn't you think that would have been enough to let me know He was still there, ready to support and guide me? No! My response was more one of surprise and doubt. Things like that didn't happen to people like me. Maybe to Mary Magdalene, doubting-Thomas or Peter—but not me. I tucked it away and told no one. After all, wouldn't they laugh and wonder if I needed to see someone "real," like a psychiatrist?

Years went by. A feeling of emptiness accompanied me. (John Bradshaw in *Bradshaw On: The Family* calls this feeling A Hole in the Soul.) There was a "hole in my soul," but I was determined to fill it with someone or something, or some accomplishment that I had achieved all by myself.

The thing that made me feel most "whole" was doing for others. I had decided that nurturing and guiding, pleasing and being the best person I could be would do it. I had already determined that to be like Jesus would be the way to go. I still hadn't gotten the message that I could actually call upon Him for guidance and support. All the Bible verses I had learned: Jesus said in Matthew 7:7 *Ask, and it shall be given you; seek, and ye shall find; knock, and it shall be opened unto you . . .* were just that to me—Bible verses. When I was angry at a loved one, how easy it would have been to follow Christ's words in Luke 23:34 *Father, forgive them; for they know not what they do.* No, I was a slow learner. I found that God has all the time in the world (and out of it). Patience is His long suit. I went on believing that even though life was hard (I was now working at two jobs, caring for my parents and trying to be a good wife and mother), I could do it all on my own.

Then God decided that it was time for another lesson. I had long ago concluded that the body wasn't important. It is what's inside that counts.

I didn't realize how important it can be as a classroom for my lessons from God. People like me, who are so sure that they can find the way all alone, seem to need "nudges" so they can really feel—physically. As Louise Hay has written, "It's often the part of the body that is affected that gives us a clue about God's intent."

God "zapped" me one morning when I was doing my monthly self-examination of my breasts. There it was, my reminder that perhaps I was expendable. After the visit to the surgeon who confirmed my fears, I readied myself for a mastectomy. When my minister visited the day after the surgery, I confided that I wished I could feel closer to God. That was all that was needed, "Just a little willingness." During the next few weeks I contracted an infection that gave me lots of time. I read books by Jampolsky, Rabbi Kurshner, the Simontons, and Bernie Siegel which reinforced my growing insight that God was telling me something, and using my body to do it. That was a turning point in my life. Rather than bitterness or anger or a feeling of "Why me?" I began to see my situation as a warning to slow down on the nurturing. After all, what's more nurturing than a breast?

Things got better for a while. I cut down on my counseling appointments. I had a woman come in to help with mother. (I still helped one daughter who was a single parent.) I worried constantly about another daughter who, with many disappointments, had tried to bring pregnancies to term. I worried about my sons' lives and whether they would find the "girl of their dreams." I had stopped my nurturing role in the more physical sense, but hadn't learned that worry, tension, and stress were just as destructive.

On the seventh day, after my second daughter, Barbara, had finally given birth to Katharine, a lovely little girl, we received a telephone call. "Katharine is dead, Mom." I didn't remember another thing for about 48 hours. Somehow, I got on a plane with Don and arrived in Atlanta where they lived. I only know on that same day I was rushed to the hospital for an operation on my brain. I spent the next month recovering at the hospital and at her house where I thought that I had come to help *her*. This is when Louise Hay's theory of the correlation between physical illness and the probable mental cause became forcefully apparent to me. It was like God was saying, in no uncertain terms, "What do I have to do to make you stop trying to be responsible for helping the whole world?" From the pain in my head it was pretty evident that He had decided to "hit me over the head!"

I slowed down a little bit again. With a wig covering my bald spot, I wobbled on weak knees to my son's wedding. Everyone said how wonderful I looked. So, I thought, "Whoopee! I'm okay. Now I can go on with my life." I think I may have mentioned I was a slow learner. The next episode God presented me with was when I had a cataract operation. Perhaps he was saying, "When are you going to open your eyes, Ann?"

I had finally learned. The only way to "fill the hole in my soul" was to realize that it was already filled with God. All I had to do was to listen to His voice saying He would teach me all things and remind me of everything that He has said to me.

Living Each Day To The Fullest

Didn't George Bernard Shaw say, "Youth is wasted on the young?" In the past, I felt that way. I look at old photographs of myself with clear smooth skin, thick shiny brown hair, lovely tall body, and realize that 50 years ago when these pictures were taken I would say to my dad, "Dad, don't take any pictures of me! I look awful!"

Now when I moan to myself about how I'm old, ugly, fat, sick and tired I stop midway and dispute my mistaken notions. Each stage of our life has its highs and lows. When you are a baby, you can't do anything. Everyone tells you what to do. You feel like it's going to be forever before you can cross the street alone. When you are in grammar school a driver's license seems eons away. When you are a teen you think you'll always be in high school and never get a job and make a lot of money. When you marry and have a family you say, "I wish I were back playing with my friends, carefree, with no responsibilities." When the children graduate you think, "Now I'll have time to play." All of a sudden you say, "Where did the time go?"

So, here I am sitting in my rocking chair, observing my children and grandchildren and beginning to realize that it's not what happens to me that is important. It's how I look at each happening that makes life what it is. I can say, "Oh, wurra, wurra, life is so tough," or I can say, "Thank you, God," for each new morning that dawns and each new experience You give me as a lesson from which to grow and learn.

After my mastectomy I decided that if I wanted to be in this world with my loved ones, and keep working on my spiritual climb, I would have to change my perceptions when negative emotions presented themselves. I had read enough to know that too much stress affects your immune system and you become ill. I wanted to live a full meaningful, productive life. I didn't want to leave this world yet. I loved people and life. I believed God had a divine plan. If part of it was to have me leave my body, that was okay. I would trust in God, whatever happened.

Heaven to me is not only walking on golden streets. It is the peace I can have right now *or* when my spirit sheds its body. The here and the hereafter are one. We are never lost to each other. My perceptions are changed. My expectations are different. I am more at peace. When something happens that really hurts I reevaluate my priorities. Life is no longer unbearable. It is now a gift.

Expectations

I was talking to my walking buddies the other day. The subject of expectations came up. I said, "Isn't it amazing that we get these weird ideas in our heads about what it's going to be like when our kids get out of school and go to work and maybe marry?" It's that "happily ever after" myth that the fairy tales told us about. It's, "Work hard and you'll get a promotion and lots of money." It's, "Be good and nothing bad will ever happen to you." It's, "Raise them right and there will be no problems."

We all agreed that we had been under the impression that our worries would be over after our children's college graduation. How naive we were! And what did we teach our children with this promised dream? Whenever anything painful came into their lives, they believed that it shouldn't be that way. Life shouldn't be hard. We passed on a false illusion that life was really a "bowl of cherries" and everyone else didn't have a care in the world. Wouldn't it have been better if we'd said, "Sometimes, life stinks!" Or possibly we could have said, "Well, that's life!"

I think that when baby Katharine died all the pain and suffering of the world became much more to me than, "Oh well, life's like that sometimes." I began to see that each hard time was a lesson sent to me from God. I realize more and more that we can find a healing lesson in every tragedy that befalls us. We can actually thank God for giving us the opportunity to advance on our spiritual path. I've also found that many people are not ready to hear about thanking God for adversity. I'm sure that when they hear about some of the hard times we've gone through some will say, "She's thanking God for that? That head operation must have made her a little crazy!" That's okay. All I have to know is that I'm a sister to every other child of God and a child of God, myself. I also must let others know that He is there, whenever they are ready. All they have to do is ask, seek, and knock.

It's Never Too Late To Change

Why do some seniors have busy, useful, and fulfilling lives while others, who are the same age and have no debilitating illness or physical condition become inactive, sedentary and often resigned to retreating from life? As I visited older friends and residents of nursing homes some common beliefs began to come together. Those who seemed to be withdrawing had a preconceived notion that at a certain age they were "old" and with this idea they added "and therefore I cannot function well." They followed that observation with "and therefore people will not want to be with me." Other conclusions were: If you are "old":

- You can't control yourself or your environment, so you'd better not do anything that would embarrass you.
- You'll do something clumsy and fall and get hurt. Then you'll be a burden to someone else.
- You won't be interesting to other people. They know so much more than you do.
- You can't be where you really want to be, so you might as well not participate.
- They put you with a whole lot of really old people and you don't want to be considered one of them.

It is never too late to encourage a senior. All the ideas just mentioned are only perceptions which are not truths written in stone. Much has been written about how our thinking actually effects our physical well being. Often, we begin to believe the myths that have abounded for years, "I've been doing things my way so long, I can't change." "Now that I'm old, I'll need service." "Everyone says old-age is awful, so why should I try to be different?" The more we believe these old stories, the more we act them out in our lives. When we go into a new stage of our life, whether it be the first day of school, a new job, marriage, divorce or getting "old," there is an element of fear that often takes a toll from our self-esteem. So we must encourage, whether it be ourselves or our seniors.

So Many Questions, All The Same Answer

Do you ever wake up in the night and feel that your head is reeling with questions? Do you feel as if you can never answer them? Maybe you've had some of the same ones flash through your mind as I have and feel the same helplessness: "What should I do about continuing my work? What should I do about my weight gain? What should I do about feeling so useless? Is this just a midwinter slump or am I suffering from depression? How can I feel as independent as I used to feel? What can I do to have fun?"

I think that somewhere I got the idea that things shouldn't change. That if I just plan and work hard enough I will be able to control my life and be happy. I need to explore this feeling. In the divine plan of life my physical, mental, emotional and spiritual life may stay at a certain plateau. It may improve and grow or become more difficult to deal with. I know there are times when I feel more alive, vital and sharp than I have in the past two years since my illness, and feel like my former self. On the other hand, at times the feelings of self-doubt overwhelm me. I remember once asking a friend about menopause. "What is it like?" I asked.

She said, "One thing you can count on is that it's never what you expect. The only thing you can be sure of is its unpredictability. The only constant is its inconsistency." As my friend described "the change," the only definite conclusion I can really come to about life is that it will change.

It doesn't matter what I do. Each situation can be a lesson in love if I allow it. Whenever I ask myself, "What shall I do?" it's my ego talking. If I can get to a point where I can automatically change that question to, "Lord, please show me the way," I will have taken a big step on my spiritual journey.

I don't need to judge whether my life is fun or fair. My body is the home in which my spirit lives while it learns God's lessons. The world is a classroom, as I perceive it. God will teach us if we are willing to learn. This is the one answer.

A New Role For Me

I have experienced the role of caregiver for my mother and father. I have lived with them through the shock, denial, confusion, sadness, anger and final acceptance that they went through as they encountered old age. I witnessed the loss of skills, bodily functions and capabilities that they once took for granted. I shared with them the bewilderment of wondering what their next life would be like. I finally had the privilege of accompanying them to the threshold of that place and time when their spirits would join God. As a result of this time of my life, I began to realize that all my experiences in teaching, counseling, being with my family were preparing me for my next step. All the physical illness I had gone through along my spiritual path had brought me to a place where I must try to share a way to create harmony between the generations based on love and encouragement.

There are so many things I'd like you to know about me. Intellectually, I know there are things I can't do any more. I am emotionally angry and sad that I can't. Now when I try, the consequences are frightening. I forget important things that used to come without even thinking about them. I make more mistakes than I used to. My body rebels when I try to do some physical activity that used to be so easy. It aches, stumbles, and shakes—it feels so uncoordinated at times. The body that was doing ballet when I was fifty and swimming laps at sixty now says, "Hold it, I'm bushed," when I complete the second walk around the block.

As I said, I have experienced being a caregiver. Now, at sixty-six, a new role emerges; I see it coming: The supermarket man's offer to give help; my grandchildren's questioning eyes when it comes to my playing baseball or splashing each other in the pool. My children's momentary frightened look when I say I have a headache. I am at a turning point where I may have to begin accepting care. I hope this is also a point at which I may observe both roles and see the beauty in each of them.

One day I helped a friend with a difficult piece she was learning to play on the piano. She offered to pay me. I said, "No, I enjoyed doing it." I will always remember her answer.

"Receiving is also a way to show love. You gave your knowledge and now I can honor you by accepting and respecting it." I hope I can do this for others.

Yes, I'm A Lefty— What's It To You?

I stood outside the 4th grade classroom, my face hot and red with humiliation. No matter how I squeezed them back into my eyes, the tears trickled down my cheeks and dripped onto the new school jumper Mom and I had bought for my first day of school. "I hate Miss Parson," I thought. Why couldn't I be like my Mom and Dad. They're normal. They're 'right-handed.' Please don't make me different, dear Lord."

I had just experienced the most embarrassing moment of my young life. "Put the pencil in your right hand, Ann. You're tilting your paper all wrong. Can't you see the other boys and girls? They're doing it right. People write with their right hands. Don't you know your left from your right?"

My head was exploding with confusion. No one had ever said anything about this before. In fact, the other teachers in the past had complimented me on my neatness and how I formed my letters. Now we were going to learn the "Palmer" method and there was only one way to do it. I couldn't! So there I was, in the hall. "I'm calling your mother right now," said Miss Parsons.

After what seemed like eons of having people pass me in the hall, smirking kids, serious-faced adults, my mother arrived. Miss Parsons sent me to sit in the principal's office. Oh, the embarrassment! Mr. Claudius was always so kind to me and I loved him.

I'll never know what happened during the next five minutes, but it was as if my Mother must have come galloping in shining armor on a beautiful white stallion and rescued me from the "Wicked Witch of the West."

Never again did I hear that I was "doing it all wrong." The W.W. of the W. came quietly to the principal's office and brought me back into the room. "You may continue as you were," she said. Never again did anyone question or criticize my penmanship.

From that moment on, I knew that I was not an abnormal freak who was "bad." I knew that it was okay to be different. Wouldn't it be wonderful if everyone could learn this lesson when they were just nine years-old? Thank you, Lord.

Some Things I Do When I Feel Stressed

Exercise

Avoid self-medication (including smoking, alcohol)

Accept what I know I can't change

Balance work with recreation

Do something for someone else

Minimize disruptions

Organize my day

Use a less crisis-like term to describe a
situation

Gather information about a concern; write
it down

Prioritize demands

Share my concerns with someone who has time

Control my anger; show love

Have compassion for myself

Draw on inner strength for solutions

Stress can be beneficial in short periods but long continued stress often leads to illness. Different things give stress to different people. Sources of stress can be physical, mental or emotional. It is often caused by the intensity of demands I or others put on me. A person may be unaware of stress and think it's a physical ailment. We often have a pattern of response: first, alarm; second, resistance; third, exhaustion; forth, illness.

Other ideas for dealing with stress:

Relaxation techniques

Good nutrition

Spiritual study

Temporary medication by a physician

Counseling

Some Activities I Enjoy Doing

As we get older we often think we don't have as much purpose in our lives as we had earlier. Our children may be grown; we may not be working outside of our home anymore. We sometimes wander around from room to room and wonder, "What shall I do that's meaningful and fun to me?"

- ♥ I like to baby-sit, but not for more than a few hours.
- ♥ I like to be included in family activities, even if I may be an observer.
- ♥ I like to write to friends and read letters from them.
- ♥ I like short visits from my children's friends.
- ♥ I like to relax and rest.
- ♥ I like to meditate and have my private daily devotions.
- ♥ I like some TV but I'm selective about my choices.
- ♥ I like to go shopping for clothes, but not take over an hour.
- ♥ I like movies, concerts, plays.
- ♥ I like to go out for dinner.
- ♥ I like to type.
- ♥ I like to read papers, magazines, fiction and non-fiction.
- ♥ I like to play cards.
- ♥ I like to exercise with the aid of a tape or in a small group.
- ♥ I like walking on a treadmill or outside when the weather is nice.

♥ I like group discussions, sometimes to lead them, sometimes as a member.

♥ I like housework—cooking, cleaning, gardening—but in small doses.

♥ I like to listen to radio, music, "living books" and tapes.

♥ I like making crafts for fairs, family and me.

♥ I like to keep mobile, even if I need a wheelchair or walker.

♥ I like to write to my congress-persons about issues, always short notes.

♥ I like to attend school events where my grandchildren participate.

♥ I like to play the piano.

♥ I like to sing in a group.

♥ I like to write in my journal.

♥ I like to swim and lie in the sun for short periods of time.

♥ I like to play tennis, but not keep score.

♥ I like to play pool, Ping-Pong, and bowl for fun.

As long as my body cooperates, there's lots to enjoy in life.

I Worry About Alzheimer's Disease

I worry about losing my memory. Ever since I had that brain operation I complain, "I'm not going to be able to think or remember anymore." It's always in the back of my mind. Even though I know fear makes things worse.

I reassure myself by listening to friends who say, "I have the same trouble. Sometimes I can't remember why I went upstairs and there are other times when I start to introduce someone and can't think of their name." Well, that's reassuring. Then I hear the new studies that say that Alzheimer's Disease is genetic or hereditary and I feel scared because a lot of the symptoms are very similar to those my grandmother had. Whenever I'm typing I always ask the Holy Spirit to help me to remember. That really helps!

For me, one way to deal with loss of memory is to make daily, weekly and monthly plans so that I will have a checklist. I wonder what would happen if Don were unable to do all the things he does to keep our life running smoothly. I know I am not supposed to live in anxiety about the future, but sometimes it's good to prepare. I don't want to be a burden to my children. I don't want to go to a nursing home unless it becomes the only alternative.

What could I put on my checklist? Chores that must be done. Meetings to which I have committed myself. Bills that must be paid. Items that have to do with my health. Hobbies. Books I want to read. Classes I would like to take. People I want to write to. Others I would like to meet for lunch, coffee or just a chat.

I think I will have to practice and learn by trial and error to find a plan which would be most helpful to me. I think a monthly calendar would help for appointments but there never seems to be enough room to put everything. I think I'll start my first checklist and use it awhile to see how it works. Don't worry if it's not like one you would like to try. You may like to go to the grocery store once a day while I may tolerate it once a week. You may prefer to have someone else do your financial work, or clean, or shop for you. It might be less stressful to plan ahead as to when these things might be accomplished by a friend or aide.

There may be some activities that will not lend themselves to pre-planning. They are governed more by the individual situation like answering letters, doctor and dentist appointments, hair cuts, car repair, furnace inspection, plumbing or electrical work. In this case it is important to record the appointments on your calendar and then after the event actually takes place to record the date it was done on your checklist.

The following is an example of a plan you might try.

Page 1. Daily Chores

Exercise

Prayer

Rest

Shower

Brush teeth

Knit

Journal

Read

Cooking

Empty trash

Check Prinny's ears

Page 2. Weekly Chores

Prayer meeting
Lawn care
Church
Go to bank
Sweep basement
Clean kitty pan
Dust
Water plants
Clean stove
Recycle
Grocery
Sweep porches
Ironing
Laundry
Day care job
Wash hair
Clean refrigerator

Page 3. Monthly Chores

Pay bills
Church nursery
Clean closets
Check for Goodwill
Sweep cobwebs
Cut toenails

Page 4. Bi-monthly Chores

Windows
Semi-monthly Chores
Caregiver meeting
Bridge club

Page 5. Extra Dates to Check

Insurance payments
Birthdays & anniversaries
Membership renewals
Driver license expiration
Car inspection expiration

All these items will be of little use unless I look at my list when I begin each day and date them each time they are accomplished. Then, perhaps I will have little need to say the statement for which my mother-in-law is famous, "I forgot to take my memory pill."

The Missing Piece of the Puzzle

In 1963 I found the first piece of the puzzle of what life's relationships are all about. I finally completed the puzzle in 1989. Twenty-six years of searching and trying to fit pieces of experience and study which sometimes would fit perfectly but often leave large spaces taunting me to get on with it! When they did fit I'd know, without a shadow of a doubt, that they were part of the answer. On the other hand, sometimes I would study them, twist them, turn them, try desperately to fit them into the big beautiful picture I was trying to see. "It's got to go together," I would say, over and over again. As I studied, worked with children in groups and counseled individuals and groups each day, my knowledge and expertise increased. But there was still something missing. There were still blank spots.

I knew all the separate pieces were parts of the whole. (I had considerable training in the Individual Psychology of Dr. Alfred Adler.) I also had become familiar with the teaching of William Glasser and his work based on a need for identity which, he believed, came from responsible living. Glasser believed that knowledge of one's own present destructive behavior could lead to change. Ah! A piece that was congruent with my belief. I got to know Carl Rogers. His deep faith in the human ability to work toward functioning more fully as a cooperative partner clicked in my brain as a definite necessity for the development of my puzzle. Albert Ellis contributed structure and humor when I worked in my haphazard but serious manner. B.F. Skinner organized me further. The Transactional Analysis of Eric Berne uncovered the parts played by early experiences and conclusions and gave hope for redesigning one's life map. At last, all the pieces came together. All? No! One was still missing! Oh, no! After all these years of work and concentration on forming my own philosophy of life, I was still foundering. After observing my own patterns of behavior and the actions of others, a gaping hole sat in the middle of my puzzle, surrounded by mounds of factophilia, separate and useless, unable to coalesce into a vibrant, complete picture of my belief.

What could I do to fill this space, this feeling of lack, this emptiness? I could do nothing. For years I had heard "Psychology and religion don't go together. One is technical, task-oriented, a science of the mind. The other is mystical, emotional, based on a personal need."

"Then why," I asked, "do so many of us feel such a compelling need to explore both. And why do we so often find relief from pain by the implementation of both?"

On the day Katharine, our seven day-old granddaughter, died I must have decided, subconsciously, that I would not stay in a life so cruel and full of pain. The doctor told my family, who had flown to Atlanta that day, that I might not live through the night. With a broken blood vessel in my brain, I was unaware of life around me. That was when God came to me in a flood of white light. He was the completion of my life puzzle. Knowing the truth, the presence of a higher being who was always there to call upon, was the missing piece that completed my puzzle of life. On that day all the pieces united and since then my prayer has been, "Lord, help me to remember that nothing is going to happen to me today that you and I together can't handle."

Why? And What Can I Do?

Today is a day when all my faith and beliefs are tested. All that I have come to know as the truth is saying to me, "Prove it!" As I've said many times, the hardest part of my life is facing the pain or fear of one of my loved ones. Breast cancer has always been a concern in our family. Don's mother died from it when she was 56. My mother had it at 82 and I had it at 59. Now we're facing the possibility of it again. One of my daughters is going to have a surgeon examine a suspicious lump. Rabbi Kurshner wrote a book, *Why Bad Things Happen to Good People.* My daughter is a good person.

Intellectually, I know what I believe. Bad things are just more lessons to help us grow. Emotionally, I'm still at a stage where I say life isn't fair. I pray that my daughter will have God's inner strength and love to cope with whatever is the outcome. From my own experience in facing breast cancer, my relationship with my husband Don grew more precious and more loving. I also grew closer to God during the time I was recovering and the days thereafter. How can I impart this to my beloved daughter? It seems like a trite sermon.

I learned that whether my body is whole or scarred it makes no difference in the way my loved ones feel about me. Even if the "worst" happens, my spirit will never die or be separated from God or my loved ones. As time goes on, I am learning how to replace fear with love and forgiveness. My help comes from the Lord. I learn that I won't gain the support I needed from drugs, alcohol, clothes, food, books, people, gimmicks, or treatments. I know I can't change my daughter's circumstances by telling her of my experience with cancer. I do know, however, that the best support I can give her is to let her know I love her and am praying for her. I believe she will be able to cope with whatever happens. I am determined that I will do all I can to help find the cause of cancer. I can petition others to influence our government to finance research to find the cure. I can urge friends to self-examine and go for a mammogram. I can help dispel their fear of doing these things. I can pray to God for strength for all those facing this challenge.

A Creed, Or Greed?

Dr. Alfred Adler wrote, that the goal of an individual was to belong and be useful. He said that we all are born of equal worth and potential. If we were encouraged during the first years of our lives we would develop self-esteem and social interest. Interest in fellow human beings and a feeling of equality would result in a productive, thriving community.

What is happening to our country? Was the writer wrong? Have the people changed? If so, what has influenced this change?

Haven't there always been those who are driven by the desire for power and greed to acquire material and money at any cost? There have been the Ebenezer Scrooges, the oil tycoons, the railroad barons, the slum landlords of each generation. Sometimes we secretly envy their accumulation of wealth which, more often than not, was acquired by questionable or even openly dishonest means.

When did the tide turn? When did we begin to close our eyes to the cruel use of foreign laborers, children in sweat shops, and minorities who were trying to feed, clothe and house their families on minimum wages or "under the table" pay?

Somewhere, during our country's growth (and I question that term), we decided to look the other way. To say, "That's life." At some point we even stopped giving clothing, furniture, food and comfort to the neighbor up the street whose husband had been killed in a mine accident. Little by little we became more concerned about what our tax deduction would be from the "Goodwill" than we were moved by the smile our neighbor would have on her face when she felt our empathy and closeness.

When did the fathers of our boys begin to say to their sons, "If you want a 'good life' (i.e., lots of money) be a doctor, lawyer, or engineer." When did the mothers begin saying, "Don't go out with him. His father's nothing but a farmhand."

It certainly wasn't radio that washed our brains: Families like Vic and Sade, Pepper Young, and Fibber McGee had just enough to get by—but they were happy. Radio writers questioned what money would do.

They asked, "How can a little girl from a small mining town in West Virginia find happiness as the wife of England's richest, most handsome lord?" And we all laughed at Jack Benny's penny-pinching.

We could go on to a logical next step that it would be easy to take. Let's blame it on television. The advertisers, the script writers, the set designers, those who developed our "rich and famous" heroes and the absence of censorship. They have destroyed our families.

Let's look back at the mommies and daddys who were role models for their children. What percentage of families had dads and mothers who even watched the programs their children chose to watch, much less censored them. In our neighborhood, filled with baby-boomers, only one family refused to buy a TV set because they felt it was a bad influence. The rest of us used it, at least in part, as a welcome baby-sitter.

"But," you say, "doesn't that mean that TV is the culprit?" I don't think so. I think we parents abdicated our responsibility to set values and teach ethics. Have you ever seen parents in the toy stores at Christmas time? Which is more loving and more effective training, having two shopping carts filled with toys advertised on TV or giving two hours of your undivided time a week. What is more effective, seeing people solve disagreements with a gun or discussing solutions with a parent? What is better preparation for the future, passing down your values or your possessions?

Sure, the producers and directors of television, the writers of comic books, and the filth of "rap," the gun, liquor, and drug sellers should use their morality, their ethical standards, and their knowledge of decency, to save our generations to come. But we have listened to their words over and over again. They are not willing to sacrifice the "almighty buck." As our Bill of Rights stands now, censorship is a frightening course of action. It seems to me that we who started all this new way to view freedom of speech have an obligation to speak out to our children and grandchildren. We have too long kept our mouths shut, believing that perhaps we would be labeled "old fashioned" and it was not our place. I believe it is part of my role as a mother and grandmother to share my values with my loved ones. I must not expect them to accept my values, but hearing them may add to their store of knowledge. As they make their own decisions they may combine their drive toward independence and freedom with a balance of compassion and morality that could produce more self-reliant, self-sufficient, cooperative members of our next generation.

My New Friend Kate

He came over in the hotel lobby to talk to us. She sat quietly on one of the plush sofas, smiling at those who walked by. Compared to my 5'8" frame she seemed tiny. Her white hair glistened; her clothes were immaculate. After a few minutes of "men talk" I said, "I think I'll go sit down." My first gut-reaction was, "I wonder if she'll want to talk." Every time I had seen her before she was pushing a complicated-looking walker. It had a basket on the front, a seat between the handles, wheels, and looked quite strongly built. I didn't want her to think I was a curious onlooker. Anyway, I sat down beside her and said, "Those two, (meaning our husbands) I can't get a word in edgewise!" She laughed.

"I've given up on that," she said. We began to talk about the hotel and what activities we had enjoyed. She said she had done almost everything the hotel offered for recreation, including a fun cruise which included going to an aquarium, watching an old-fashioned play in one of the cities, and at in-between times, swimming. "I used to be in a wheel chair," she offered, "but now that I have this thing I can go as fast as anyone."

"I have two walkers at home," I answered. "One, my mother used during her last days, and one I needed after my aneurism. Both had worn us out, because we had to lift them up and down, up and down as we walked."

Kate was such a wonderful model for growing old gracefully and beautifully. Her courage and eagerness to try everything inspired me. Her interest in life and people drew others to her. Her complete sincerity and empathy built a bond of friendship in a few short hours.

After three days she said, "We're moving to another place. The type of food here has really made me ill." My heart sank.

"You know, Kate," I interjected, "I hardly ever make friends when we go on vacation. I've really enjoyed being with you. You're so easy to talk to."

She reached out and hugged me and said, "Why, that's so nice. I just felt like I knew you right away."

Another little lesson from God. Everyone has something of love and beauty within them if we just reach out to them. Thank you, Kate.

Don't Let It Rain On My Parade

I'm sitting on the balcony outside our room. It's pouring. A few minutes ago we were on the tennis court. When weather gave us warning by getting dark and windy we headed back to the hotel. It was pouring by the time we got in the door. Now what?

What is God teaching me today? That I can't control the weather? Let's talk about control. How do people get that way? Why does control seem so important to them? Is it a need to control others that motivates them. Is it self-control? Is it control of their environment? I think it's different for each person. Perhaps they had experienced a humiliation or embarrassment so crushing that they vowed to do everything in their power to avoid having that happen again. It could have happened by chance. It could have been intentionally planned by another person. It could have been the result of their own actions. Whoever the instigator, this is how they determined they would cope—by trying to control life. If it were the fault of another (as some see it) one would subconsciously decide that her plan should be to try to control others. This could be done by physical force, holding the purse strings, or even "mind games." It could be done by threatening withdrawal of love or by subtle manipulation. Each time a situation which might be humiliating would present itself she could test the belief she held by dealing with it by trial and error, then conclude that control of others was the answer. Each time she drew this conclusion she would reinforce her original belief. She may consider two paths of action. One may be to always control others. The other may be to avoid being controlled by others. She will know which of these is most important to her by measuring her anger in conflict situations.

If, on the other hand, our heroine believed that it was her actions that brought embarrassment and humiliation, her feelings of self-worth could be left broken and bleeding. Self-blame can destroy confidence and courage. It can say, "I won't try, I might make a mistake and look like a fool." It can cause us to measure our self-worth only by the approval or disapproval of others. It can petrify us to the point where we are immobile, unable to take any risks, unable to make ourselves the judge of our own behavior and encourage ourselves. Our only hope, then, is to keep ourselves rigidly under control, treat our inner spirit as a shackled slave and tyrannize our own bodies.

Let's look at the third possibility. What if I look at life and the world as something that should be under control. What if I have it all figured out that life should always be taken care of for me. Everything has been predictable and easy and my parents took care of all my needs. They felt sorry when things were hard for me. They thought it was unfair. How angry I can be now when the world doesn't fit my plans!

Going back to the tennis and the rain. What will give me peace? What will give my partner encouragement? Certainly not being angry at the world. Not feeling sorry for myself or blaming my partner.

Replacing anger with an acceptance of life, myself and my brother or sister can give me back a feeling of fulfillment and happiness. Seeing all kinds of life experiences, and all others and myself as having equal worth, can provide a harmonious life for all.

I Didn't Sleep A Wink Last Night

I awakened at 4:00 AM. I don't know why. It doesn't matter. Years ago a teacher of mine said, "If you can't sleep, don't worry about it. Just decide what you want to do and do it." Since then I have learned that there are many reasons for insomnia. They can be physical or psychological. They can be as simple as not needing as much sleep as we used to. I think that must be mine. Whatever it is, I believe that the most important element in this situation is how I perceive it.

In the "old days" I used to toss and turn. I would dwell on how I could possibly get through the coming day. I would listen to Don snore and think, "It isn't fair. He sleeps right through the night." I would count sheep. I would do relaxation exercises. I would have a cup of warm milk or tea or eat carbohydrates or protein or whatever was the popular remedy of the month. Did they work? Of course not. I was depending on something outside myself. My God, who could have helped me, was not consulted.

I shouldn't have said, "God, make me go to sleep." I now know that my hours of tossing and turning in misery could have been turned into peace just by asking for help in coping. I know that spending a few minutes with Him could have led me to a solution. I could have reminded myself to be still and allow His help to flow through my mind until I would either have the answer or be asleep. Now since I have found this beautiful key, there have been no more turbulent nights. I still wake up, but now I lie quietly and communicate with God. I respectfully request His presence. I give my problems to Him. I wait to be moved. I don't think actively. I become a vessel into which God pours his loving answer and then I act. Action can be all kinds of exciting things. It can be prayer, reading, writing, counting my blessings, or just lying quietly and being in a state of bliss for just being alive. Thank you, God, for this wonderful lesson.

A Trip To Paradise

We awakened at 2:00, 3:00 and 4:00 AM. I was so afraid that we'd miss the plane that I set two alarms! Right now I'm sitting on a little beach in a secluded cove. A water-fall cascades down the rocks. We've been wanting to come to Bermuda for years. It's everything I ever expected. Don's out exploring. He always has to get to know a place the first day. He studies all the sight-seeing opportunities, walks and fills every minute. I sit and soak up the sun, the scenery and the water, the peace. Opposites do attract! I can see the ocean from my chair. It sparkles with a beauty I can't de-scribe. People reveal themselves and I get to know them by their actions. A group of men stand together attempting to out-do each other with their stories of shock and violence. "Oh, yeah, he fell asleep on the beach and wound up in the hospital. They drugged him and took his Rolex."

Women light cigarettes and sip from their rum swizzles at 11:00 AM. Children throw sand at each other and quickly look away to avoid their parents' eyes. Here and there a relaxed body reclines, absorbing God's creation, but ego speaks everywhere.

At the breakfast table this morning Don was talking about a book he was reading about the history of Massachusetts. He was commenting on how different ethnic groups back in the 1700s had to prove they were the best. Has life changed so much? If only we could all change our goals to proving how we can live together, cooperate and show caring. How would the world be different? We would need no wars. Sports would be played to demonstrate skill, strength, agility and character, not to show who was best. We talked about a team we both enjoy watching. They are high in the standings but didn't get there because of their best players being bought for the highest amount of money. They are in that position, I think, because of loyalty to their fans, friendship with other players on their team, and a real enthusiasm for the game.

So why have I called this Paradise? I decided, after receiving some abrupt answers, averted eyes, glassy stares and frowns that I would test a phrase I had heard. It was "giving is receiving." I wondered what would happen if I greeted each person I met (whether it be an employee of the hotel or a guest) with a smile and a salutation such as "good morning" or a comment about an event we were sharing. It was like looking through "love-colored" glasses.

Each person became a beloved child of God. The unconditional love God poured through me, passed in wider and
wider circles like ripples on a pond, back to me and on to
others. With a little willingness from me to show love, God
had created a paradise.

Part 3

Finding Peace Between The Generations

Seasons

As a sparkling brook swells to sing
the melodies of a dawning world,
love grows. It soars with the ecstasy
of discovery on the wings of youth.

A ray of light reflects the forest's
nursery. Extending into heaven,
it searches the earth's shadow and
glimmers in passionate perception.

Above a fallen nest of golden fields
the sky burns in vintage red.
Nature's harvest shines as autumn's
wisdom dances upon the horizon.

A cool breeze flurries in the twilight.
Scattering ashes and exciting embers,
it draws years into moments of
vivid experience and feeds the flames.

Seasons change as the seasons of man.
To glance past winter is to drink
the dew of rebirth. To gaze past
age is to realize the visions of love.

Thomas Tuites

(Dedicated to his grandparents on their 50th anniversary.)

This Is My Mom

I wrote a tribute to mom and put it in a frame beside her bed at the nursing home. I read it to her many times during her last days.

Dear Mom,

You have shown me what courage is when you're in pain or afraid.

You have taught children and shown them a love of learning.

You have enabled hundreds of Girl Scouts to grow and learn.

You have kept three English children safe from harm during the war.

You helped Dad become a leader in Eastman Kodak Company.

You provided a beautiful home for me during my youth and for Dad for 63 years.

You brought joy to many, many friends for 92 years.

You were the beginning of a child, four beautiful grandchildren and five great grandchildren.

You gave your devotion, service and money to your church, whenever they were needed.

You are an example of strength, wisdom, peace, joy, forgiveness, love, patience, acceptance, understanding, harmony, healing, humor, protection, compassion, comfort, courage, confidence for me, always.

For all this you must hold a great pride and happiness always in your heart, for you live life as a true child of God.

With love and admiration, always,

Ann

It seems to me that when we're sitting around talking about our loved ones, we aren't talking about real people with real feelings anymore. We're talking about how hard life is for us. We're talking about how to pay the bills. Sometimes it turns into an "ain't it awful" session. We feel frustration and anger at the person who, for many years, may have cared for us and raised us in the best way they knew.

It may be that this is a way that we distance ourselves from them as we prepare to let go. It may be that as they go through this last difficult stage of their lives they change and we don't know them as the same people or how to communicate with them anymore.

Let's consider a new way to look at these loved ones. Stop for a moment and try to see their every bid for attention, power play, attack (physical or verbal), withdrawal, as a cry for help, a plea for love. See this person as a part of you and a beloved child of God. The moment you change your perception of this person your actions and attitude may also change. Anger cannot exist when love is present. The powerful energy of love will engulf you and as you give it you will also receive it.

What is love? Or what isn't it? It's not service. It's not submitting to demands. It's not overindulging. It's not overprotecting, or just saying, "I love you." It's accepting others just the way they are. It's forgiving the past. It's not expecting anything in the future. It's having unconditional positive regard for others.

During the last few months of my Mother's life, it was painful for both of us. There was confusion, hurt and fear that we might part before we closed the great chasm that had grown between us. At that time I read, *Love is Letting Go of Fear* by Gerald Jampolsky. I learned that all I had to do was love and forgive and peace would come. I decided to give love in spite of the punishment heaped upon me because Mom interpreted my action as abandoning her. I decided to give her unconditional love.

This was a very frightening time for me. I was torn between doing what I believed God would want me to do and feeling that I was overstepping all boundaries of what the role of a respectful, caring daughter should be. Wasn't it presumptuous to tell mother what I believed about life after the death of the body? Was it an act of love? I decided to follow my inner voice. I would let her know what I believed, and yet not try to force her to do the same. Over and over, I would say, "God loves you and forgives you. Dad loves you and forgives you, I love you and forgive you. All your friends and family love you and forgive you. When your spirit leaves your body God will receive you in his loving arms. There will be no more pain. We will all be with you, always." The more I waited, patiently and peacefully, and conveyed these thoughts to her, the more my faith strengthened. Even when she was unable to respond and seemed to be sleeping during the last weeks of her life I would continue to let her know how she was loved by God, her friends and family.

Many of the times when I visited the nursing home, where she had to be when I was physically unable to care for her, she wouldn't look at me or speak to me. After days of stony silence she asked, "Why do you keep coming back when I'm so mean?" I told her I loved her. To me, this was a turning point for us. During her last days, one night as I sat and held her hand she opened her eyes and spoke to me, "Oh, Ann, I do love you." What a joy it was for me to know that we had come to that closure before she left her body. Being with Mother those last months was another lesson given to me on my spiritual journey. The lesson for me was to learn by making a promise to live with patience, love and forgiveness. As I sat with mom I saw her anger at her illness turn, day by day, to these powerful emotions and finally to peace.

When you are close to someone who is terminally ill there are things you may want to share. I believe that my mother needed to learn that death is not failure. For two years in the nursing home mom knitted, wrote letters, washed and dressed herself. She went to the chapel in her wheelchair on Sunday. She walked up and down the hall each day with the help of her walker and my arm. She read magazines and watched TV. At the end of those two years, when she was no longer able to do any of these things, she began to sleep more and more. She ate less and less. It was almost as if she were preparing to go. She'd be calm and cooperative and loving but it seemed as if she were on her way. As she grew less responsive I would talk to her about how all the family members and her friends loved her. I'd talk about happy times she and Dad had had together and funny things she had experienced with her grandchildren. I would hold her hand and tell her that we would always be together. I told her of a forgiving God. I know that she heard me. She became more and more peaceful. She was ready to meet the Lord. The nurse came in. I said, "She's gone." The nurse was a lovely young woman who wasn't quite sure what to do. I said, "It's okay, she's with God, she just left her body." I said a prayer of thanksgiving that she was now without pain and at peace. Her miracle of life had occurred.

My Dad

I never really knew my dad. I wanted to, oh, how I wanted to. I didn't really know what a god was, but as a little girl I was sure he must be one. I didn't see him much. He was out 'til all hours, helping create a new process to make color pictures, instead of black and white ones. But there was never a question in my mind that I was being taken care of and safe. His strong arms sheltered me from inclement weather, frightening things like barking dogs, big trucks and the dark. At bedtime he would come into my room, listen to my prayers, and kiss me goodnight.

Once when I was at my grandmother's house, some-one gave me a rose. As I got in the car to go home I got it caught in the door and the stem broke. Everyone "carried on" about how sad it was that the stem had broken. In my little squeaky four year-old voice I said, "That's all right; my daddy will fix it!" They all laughed; but I didn't. I knew he could do anything.

Another time when I was about eight we were driving over a bridge in Chicago in the midst of an enormous bliz-zard. At the center of the bridge the car made a complete turn. Mother and Father sat like statues, paralyzed with fear. Finally, Mother asked, "Weren't you afraid, Ann?" I an-swered in a calm voice, "No, Daddy was driving."

As the years passed, Dad made strong demands for perfection in everything I attempted to do. These were met with rebellion during my teen years. My dad's last years were full of pain caused by arthritis and degenerative hips. Although he was rarely able to express it in words, I never questioned his love. As the years passed he became more quiet and serious. In the hospital, before he died, I made sure I told him how much I loved him and that he was the best dad in the world. I was glad I told him, because that night when I returned to the hospital after going home for dinner the head nurse came to me and said, "Your father has just passed away."

Did I say I never really knew my dad? That's not true. He never talked about feelings, but he *showed* his love for me. I *knew* him.

So, tonight, on the anniversary of your passing I want to talk to you again. The longer you're away from me the more I love you and understand our relationship. Your generation was less complex to figure out. They were clear and their rules were based on ethics, morals, honesty, pride in their work, and striving toward perfection. I wish we could have talked more. You worked hard at Eastman Kodak Company and at home. You cared about me and for me but didn't say much except as the trainer and authority. You came a long way from the little town of Ravena, New York.

Did you always yearn for the two boys you and Mom lost at birth? I wish you could have held them in your arms, watched them grow, and taught them all the things a growing boy needs to learn. I always wanted those brothers, but it wasn't meant to be. As I look back, I know I was the one who perceived my lack, not you.

Thank you for being there for me, loving me and being proud of me. As I said back in the hospital that night 10 years ago, "You were the best Dad in the world."

Love, *Ann*

Planning For The Future—
Some "Ground Rules"

Perhaps the time has come when you have exhausted all avenues to allowing your elderly loved one to live independently. The decision has been made for you. Financially speaking, there is no way that you can provide the environment and the level of care that your dependent senior needs. Before the actual move, whatever you can do to plan ahead will make it easier to have a harmonious, peaceful life together. Some areas of concern must be brought out in the open and dealt with immediately.

Over and over we've read that one of the deepest problems affecting a marriage is money. This is often a huge "bone of contention" when combining two generations in one home. As seniors, we are often terrified about not having enough money to pay the bills; how we will eat, live, and take care of ourselves when we are ill. No matter how well each family has gotten along during the years when we've lived separately, we seniors hesitate to hand over the reins of our finances to anyone. The "Catch 22" is that we may find that it's more difficult to balance our checkbook and we're misplacing letters that need attention and bills that need to be paid. Although we've always trusted our children, we still think of them (even though they may be well over 30) as children.

There are many possibilities to explore as alternatives. The senior may ask a "child" who has had experience in financial planning and conservative investment to work with her. On the other hand, in order to avoid any potential of favoritism, the senior may want to deal with an unbiased, objective accountant who is not related to the family. While this may clear the air of any hurt feelings, it also will take money that could have been used for living expenses. Together, you may develop a business-like agreement, including charges for room and board and in keeping in line with the senior's ability to pay. The most important element in the planning stage is to keep the dialogue open. The goal must be, "How can we work together in accord?" rather than "Who will win?"

Should some areas of the home be earmarked specifically for certain members of the family? For instance, if teenagers are involved, is there a bath that could be used exclusively by the senior member so that conflict over the amount of time used could be side-stepped? Is there a small area where the new resident could sit, perhaps with a small television and radio so that she could still exercise her preference for programming, music or quiet, without disrupting habits of the other members of the family?

If the senior cannot be left alone, do you have friends or a reliable agency that you can count on for respite care (to give you free time each week to avoid burnout)?

A family meeting is one of the most effective means of planning ahead and dealing with problems in a democratic manner. A definite time should be set aside each week. All should be invited to attend. If one refuses, it is assumed that he will abide by the decisions made by the group. Each opinion is of equal value and each person has the right to be heard. The purpose is to find plans and solutions that are mutually satisfactory to the majority. Meetings should be brief so that those with short attention spans will not become bored or restless. It is important that no decision is "written in blood" in order that after a short period (usually a week) it can be reevaluated. Suggestions given should be taken seriously and genuine interest shown to all participants. Each person should be treated with the respect one would show a friend. Having a procedure for planning and solving problems can avoid much heartache.

My goal in writing this book is not to find ways to change your senior. It is not to make him or her do what you want. It is not to save your inheritance. There are no tricks or gimmicks. Its sole purpose is to help your family find peace while living together. It is to help you keep your sanity while the medical profession keeps the older generation alive. As is often the case, men of "progress" create a product and then realize that they don't know what to do with it. Don't keep me alive unless your motive is that we experience each other's loving presence as long as we can. Don't keep me a stranger in the land. Keeping me alive without a "plan" may be no favor to either of us. The more we know of each others' idiosyncrasies, beliefs, values, opinions, the more we can accept each other as unique individuals. If we spend some time (before the crisis of dependency occurs) in getting to know each other, we will find the achievement of harmony an easier process to undergo.

My Caregiver Group

If you ever get to a place in your life when you feel hopeless about either you, or someone you love growing old, I pray you will find a haven as I have that will give you comfort, a feeling of peace, warmth, and oneness. That haven is my "Caregiver" group. You may wonder why, since my father has been gone for seven years and my mother for three, I still go to their meetings. I guess part of it is that I got so much from it in my days of darkness that I want to give the love and encouragement I received back. It may be the close friends I made who can tell each other anything in confidence and know they will be accepted and understood. It may be when we identify with the little stories about our care receivers there is a comic relief that relaxes us and gives us hope.

Everyone is welcome. Our group meets in our church but those who attend represent all religions and ages. They are those who care for the elderly, a relative or spouse with a serious illness. These meetings are held in a home, church, nursing home, wherever it's convenient. They are open to all.

Sometimes we spend the whole meeting going around the room getting caught up on members' situations. Sometimes, one person needs to talk for a long time. Somehow, there is no resentment toward this and all center on giving support for the one who is speaking.

What are some things we do? We allow a person to ventilate—get his concerns out in the open, and realize that he's not alone. About every other time we have speakers who help with specific areas, such as finances, legal areas, health care, Medicare or Medicaid information, home health aides, respite care, and nursing home exploration. We learn about techniques of encouragement and spiritual support if it is requested.

On the theory that "many heads are sometimes better than one" we brainstorm to find new options to help solve individual situations. Many times a shared experience will present a new idea never considered before. The gift I receive each time I attend is learning how I can be more cooperative when I reach this time of life and need care, myself.

As I have lived the life of a caregiver, I can try to remember and "walk in my helper's moccasins." As one of my friends in the group said recently, "I would have landed in the nuthouse if it hadn't been for you guys." I especially want to give a prayer of thanksgiving for our leader who has continually given her devoted service year after year.

Why Do We Misbehave?

Why do I act so badly at times? Those around me think, "She didn't used to be this way." I'm not trying to justify my behavior or make excuses, but I think I've found a pattern. It seems to be that I "act up" when I feel most afraid or discouraged. My angry, resentful, lonely child within is confused and frustrated and especially fearful, even to the point of giving up at times. When I feel like this I try all ways to find my place of belonging again. I know I did have it once. I was useful, productive, caring and giving. Now I find that things aren't the same. I'm not able to do the things I used to do. My children are grown and have their own lives. I'm "too old" for a job. I can't keep up my home so I may have to live in a new place. When I wake up in the morning so many things flash through my mind. I'm near the age when my parents died. Some of my friends have died. I try to do everything right, the way I used to do and I hardly ever measure up anymore. I feel I've got to keep things under control. Concerning death—I don't know what it's going to be like. I don't like things that are unknown. But I know that when my body dies I (my spirit) will be with the Lord. And that will be worth it all. Often I'm angry at the unfairness of life. As this happens, we older people tend to be in a constant state of fear. Life in this world becomes more and more frightening and we seniors begin to blame ourselves or others for the predicament in which we perceive ourselves to be. When I feel this way I find myself doing all sorts of things that aren't the "old me."

I misbehave:

- I try to get more attention, even though I know that the person "taking care" of me is already up to her ears in raising her family, working and trying to cope with each day. I've become so self-centered. It's a matter of life and death to me and more important than anyone else's problems.

- I try to control my life, but in doing so I often make it harder for those around me. I become more demanding because I think maybe I can get someone else to make things better.
- I do or say hurting things to get back at the unfairness in life. But in doing so I hurt those who are trying to help me. I lash out and hurt those I love.
- I give up. I feel helpless, so I just sit or lie in my bed and don't respond to anyone. I withdraw, especially if I'm trying to solve my problems without God's help.

What can you do when I "pull" these things? When I demand more attention than is due me, don't fall for it. Give me attention when you can. Spend a few minutes. Share what's going on outside my room. Sit with me when you write a letter or do other work. I'll try not to interrupt.

When I try to be in control, let me know that it is your home. Don't let me pull you into an argument. Don't try to control me; just be firm and friendly and honest.

When I say things that hurt you, refuse to be hurt. Realize that I'm angry at life and "you always hurt the one you love."

When I feel hopeless, don't give up on me. Let me know that you believe I can cope, no matter how hard life seems for me. I don't want your pity. I don't want to keep secrets.

I don't want to play games. I don't want to worry about what others think. I want to be me. I want you to be you.

The "Terrible Twelve"

Long ago, when I was teaching and leading parenting groups I came across a list called the "Typical Twelve" in a book by Thomas Gordon called *Parent Effectiveness Training*. As the years went by I think we changed the title to the "Terrible Twelve" because we realized, more and more, how discouraging these actions were to children. Later, we discovered that they applied to anyone, not just children.

Today, as I was talking to my daughter about her twelve year-old son I said, "If we don't tell him what to do and how to do it, he'll finish his work and do it well. I just hope he gets in a line of work where he doesn't have a boss."

My daughter answered, "Or a job where the boss allows him to do his work in his own way." Then she said, "I guess everyone would like it to be that way."

I've been thinking about that. So I decided to share the "Terrible Twelve" with you. As a senior citizen:

- I don't like to be *ordered* or *commanded* to do something. It makes me feel inferior and stupid.
- I don't like to be *warned* or *threatened*. I feel pressured and fearful.

- I don't like to be *preached* at. It makes me feel that I'm a bad person.
- I don't want you to give me a *solution*. I feel like you don't think I can solve my own problem.
- I don't like to be *lectured*. I feel belittled and dumb.
- I don't like to be *blamed*. I feel defensive and victimized for something I often haven't done.
- I don't like to be *praised*. I feel I'm being patronized.
- I hate being called *names*. The bad ones shame and the "good" ones embarass me.
- I don't like to be *analyzed*. I feel like you're talking about someone else and that I'm not a person.
- I hate *sympathy*. I think I must be a person others feel sorry for and pity.
- I don't want you to *question* or *interrogate*. I feel like I'm being cross-examined.
- Please don't *withdraw* and *not talk* to me. It terrifies me.

Six Basic Elements Of Encouragement

So, what can we do to replace the "Terrible Twelve?" Don Dinkmeyer and Lewis Losoncy wrote in a book called *The Encouragement Book* about ways to become more positive while becoming more encouraging to others. There are six attitudes of encouragement that not only help us grow but also help others increase their self-esteem.

As a senior citizen, this is how I'd like to be treated:

♥ *Acceptance*—Accept me the way I am. I'm doing the best I can. Anything negative you say to me makes my feeling of worth plunge. Anything positive gives me hope in this time of discouragement.

♥ *Empathy*—Try to walk in my shoes and see how I'm feeling. If you show understanding, I won't feel so "out of step."

♥ *Enthusiasm*—If I accomplish anything, let me know I'm of use. If I have an idea, let me know if there's any merit in it.

♥ *Confidence*—Believe in me. Let me know that you think I can make it through this difficult time of my life. Be optimistic.

♥ *A non-blaming attitude*—Concentrate on the problem, not on identifying the culprit.

♥ *Listen, without evaluating*—Let me know that you have heard me.

Not Guilty

I went to my "Caregiver" meeting last night. I couldn't help but notice how the room was filled with feelings of guilt. I thought to myself, "These people are here because they want to improve the relationship they have with their senior." It kind of reminded me of the story of the preacher who exhorts the loyal members who come out every Sunday regardless of weather, illness or vacation time to "Come to church."

Why were these loving and unselfish people, whose lives were permeated with giving and altruism, feeling guilty? Feeling guilty and being guilty are not the same. It comes from demanding more from themselves.

I believe there is such a division, especially in the minds of those who have not experienced a situation of care-giving. Their comments invite huge guilt trips on the part of caregivers. Some are convinced that putting your senior into a retirement home or a nursing home is an admission of failure or a declaration of moral bankruptcy. Their comments often indicate a judgment of laziness, self-centeredness or indifference on the part of the caregiver. On the other hand, when I kept my mother and father in my home for many years, others would infer, most subtly, that I was weak because I didn't stand up for my rights. Often they hinted at my desire to save the money (that my parents might have used for care) for myself. As our leader said one night, "You're wrong no matter what you do."

Doesn't it all boil down to how each caregiver really feels and what the real needs of the situation are?

A young man I know visits his mother each night in the nursing home and helps her do her physical therapy. Another caregiver, an only child, has quit her job and spends day and night caring for her mother at home. Should either one feel guilty? Is there any right or wrong solution? Isn't it all in the mind, heart and spirit of each caregiver? Maybe they are guilty of loving too much. Truthfully, though, anyone ever love too much?

Anger

When someone says or does something that conflicts with our belief system we experience anger. Often there is a sense of unfairness. When this happens we have a decision to make. Do we want to use the anger to solve the problem, or do we want to use love and forgiveness? A decision to use anger perpetuates the feeling of conflict and stress. A decision to use love and forgiveness drives out the anger and feelings of blaming and desire to "hurt back." Staying in the emotion blocks solution. Deciding on a positive cooperative mutual solution works towards peace and cleanses us of stress. It drives out anger. Feelings of love and anger cannot exist together. Here's what to do:

- ♥ Find out why we're angry. Check old tapes, hurts, parental injunctions. Go on from there. It's only the first step, and it won't help to use these as an excuse for our behavior.
- ♥ Think of the needs of the whole situation by observing it as objectively as we possibly can.
- ♥ Look at all pros and cons to find the best solution for all parties.
- ♥ Enlist the aid of our perceived adversary. We must concentrate on how we can find a mutual solution rather than on who is going to win this conflict.

Paula and her mother are so tense and upset that they can hardly contain their anger. Paula's mother's husband has left her but keeps threatening to come back and take things from the home. Paula is frightened for her mother's safety and stays close to her. Paula's mother feels trapped. She has no time for privacy or independence. They wind up screaming at each other and at Paula's children. Paula feels her mother should be grateful for the protection Paula gives. A loving relationship of many years has come to an impasse. How could we put the above steps into practice to break this barrier?

Relinquishing Parental Power

For a long time, Miss Claudia was the authority in her home. The children listened because she was the parent. Then one day they didn't listen anymore. (She was now living at her son's home.) Sometimes they laughed at her old-fashioned ideas. She felt rejected and angry. She would quote the verse in the Bible "Honor thy father and thy mother . . . " (Exodus 20:12) and say, "Listen here, young man, you've got to show me respect. I'm your mother!"

Miss Claudia didn't realize that in a democratic family where everyone wants to feel of equal worth, you don't automatically get respect just because you're bigger, strong or older or believe that you're the boss. Everyone must ea respect by their actions.

Living in a democratic family, as the mother, I learned very early that, "Just because you're older doesn't give you the right to be boss." We taught this principle to our children and, having done this, had to live by it, too. Age doesn't automatically mean power. It doesn't mean wisdom. It only means these things if you work toward maturity and cooperation. It gives no one the right to expect compliance or obedience or esteem.

I guess one of the reasons we seniors feel so sure that we "know best" is what we believe to be our vast experience. We don't consider that every person has different experiences which mean different things when added to a totally unique lifestyle. What one person might learn might be entirely different from conclusions made by someone else.

Another little "gem" I have collected along the way is: If my friends or family want advice or my opinion on some subject, they will ask for it. Telling people what to do or not to do is a sure-fire way to get the opposite results.

What can we do? When we are living in someone else's home we can take care of our own belongings. We can offer help. We can decide, when invited, if we will join the family or if we will do something we enjoy in our own room. We must give up any semblance of authority we may have had during our parenting years. Mutual respect is the answer.

Maintaining Routine

Grandma Mary had always had a schedule when she lived on the farm. Now, at her daughter's house, life was different. Grandma would stay in bed long after she awakened so as not to bother anyone. Even then, some days they all ate breakfast together or her daughter and son-in-law stopped for breakfast on the way to work. Some days they wanted to drop her at the Senior Center. "I don't know why she can't be ready," her son-in-law would say. "She doesn't have anything else to do."

Grandma Mary's new family needed a way to inform her about their plans. She is used to getting up early so being ready is not the problem. "A routine for the week would help the confusion," she thought. If her daughter and son-in-law like more spontaneity, they could at least post a schedule for the following day where she could easily see it. Since seniors occasionally forget, even when they are told, a brief note such as "Dr. Brown, 2:00 PM tomorrow" would avoid last minute tension.

A daily routine during the week could eliminate family conflict. Having certain days for doing laundry, errands, having visitors and meals, rising and going to bed, could help us to know what is expected of us and give us a sense of security. Weekends can be a time to relax routine, but even then it is important to let the senior know what is expected of her. Each family must work out a routine that will meet the needs of the family as a whole. If the daughter and son-in-law (as in Grandma Mary's case) want to have company just for themselves, they should say so. "John and I are having the Smiths over tonight and we will bring you your dinner when it is ready." If Grandma is offended this can often be avoided by preparing her earlier at a family meeting. "There are times when all of us want private times with our friends."

There is no fixed calendar or time schedule that fits every family. In order to find the most fulfilling routine, it is often effective to meet together and gather information from each member. When the needs of all members are considered, no one should be offended.

Taking Time For Training

Mary Ann's mother, an excellent homemaker, had raised four girls. Now, she was doing things that shocked Mary Ann. Mother would help around the house, assuring Mary Ann that she could do the job. Later in the day Mary Ann would find dirty dishes in the cupboard and dirty silverware put back in the drawer. She mentioned to her mother that maybe her eyes weren't as good as they used to be and perhaps she should wait for Mary Ann to do the dishes. Her answer was, "I can see just fine. They weren't used so I put them back."

Mary Ann watched to see if it continued. When it did, she would remove the dirty dishes and silverware and re-wash them so she wouldn't hurt her mother's feelings. This may have worked except that while Mary Ann was following this course of action frustration and anger were building up inside her—with no outlet. Mother really believed that she was helping. In order to correct the situation, Mary Ann could have taken some time to explain how the work was done in her home. She could have said, "After we eat, we put all the dishes and utensils by the dishwasher. Then Bobby loads the dishwasher. Thank you for carrying them over to the shelf."

Jean's Aunt Agnes lived with her. She would "help" while Jean was at work. She would put a load of clothes in the washer. Jean would come home and find a pink load of washing because a red shirt had gotten in with the white clothes. Jean knew that older people need to feel useful so she asked if Aunt Agnes would separate the clothes into color piles, but then leave them for Jean to wash when she came home. She also asked Aunt Agnes to fold the dry clothes for her. If appreciation continues to be shown with a genuine desire to have help, Aunt Agnes will become a real asset to Jean.

Very often a caregiver hesitates to discuss mistakes with her elder. This is guaranteed to increase tension, be-cause resentment and hostility will store up inside until they explode. At that time the senior won't understand and the relationship will become strained.

Training should never be done in the heat of a situation where a mistake has been made. It should not be done when anger is present. It should never be done in the presence of friends or neighbors.

One of the most difficult times a senior must face is when she/he has trouble remembering where things are, appointments, or what someone has asked her to do. To rectify this problem, the caregiver should take time to set up a simple system of writing down the location of important papers, jewelry or other items that the senior uses. A large calendar can be put in a prominent place and the senior and caregiver can keep it up-to-date together. Also, a notebook and pencil for taking messages can be placed next to the telephone. Writing things down can be extremely important. The senior can be taught that it's all right to take time to write. If you discover that she doesn't take messages accurately, you may have to ask her not to answer the phone. You could then arrange for an answering device to take your messages when you are away.

Training can be accomplished by means other than just talking to someone. Dan's father was diabetic, and not able to have candy or alcohol. These were two of his favorite things, so he would follow orders—except when Dan and the family were out of the house. Dan spoke to his father about how this would effect his health. He asked him if he would like to have Dan do anything different to help him. They explored all sorts of alternatives—from not having these items in the house, locking them up, in order to help Dan's father take responsibility for his own health. Working together on a solution was encouraging to both men. They could try out different plans, then evaluate their success. As a result, Dan's father felt he was being treated as an equal rather than a "bad boy" who must be punished.

Minimizing Mistakes

Great Aunt Laura was determined that she would help during her visit with her niece. Laura had always been a good cook, so she decided to make a pie for her niece. Granted, she was a little shaky and tired easily, but she'd do it. The crust was ready and she began to pour the filling into it. Then, the bowl slipped. "Auntie, what a mess!" cried her niece. "Never mind, I'll clean it up. I told you I'd be glad to make the meals while you are visiting me!" Laura was saddened.

When we get to this time in our life we are already questioning our worth. We know that we aren't as efficient as we used to be. We want to maintain our confidence and keep trying even though our body often does not cooperate. Criticism often means that you have lost faith in the senior. Dr. Rudolph Dreikurs, a leader in child psychiatry said, "A mistake is a friendly invitation to try again." Even at advanced age, it is never too late to try again. We can learn from our mistakes. The more you point out weaknesses, the more discouraged a senior becomes. Great Aunt Laura needed to hear what a beautiful pie crust she had made and how thoughtful it was that she wanted to surprise her niece. Now it will be difficult to attempt anything with Laura's growing fear of failure which was reinforced by this episode.

Grams loved to knit but her eyesight was failing and her hands wouldn't stay still. She talked about it with her daughter. They decided on a plan whereby Grams could knit squares to put together for legwarmers for the people in the nursing home. If she made a mistake, she would leave it for her daughter to repair when she got home. As a result, Grams felt useful and didn't dwell on all the beautiful sweaters she *used* to make for her family. The main idea is not to concentrate on the mistake, but what we can do about it and what we might learn from it. You don't have to point out what I'm doing wrong—I already know that!

Identifying The Issue— Dealing With The Problem

Gram's hearing was beginning to deteriorate. She didn't hear every word, especially when there were many people around. She seemed to be able to handle "one on one," when facing them. But certain tones bothered her. Often, she didn't get the content or meaning. When she tried to answer, it often sounded funny and people would laugh. Grams knew it because they became embarrassed and didn't know what to say. It made her so humiliated that she tended to withdraw, not wanting to talk anymore. At least that way she wouldn't make another mistake. She would try to remember to say, "I'm sorry, I didn't hear you." But it was happening so often now that even that embarrassed her.

When this happens to a loved one the best we, as caregivers, can do is to first get professional advice from a doctor. It may be something as simple as a buildup of wax. Or, it could be something that could be corrected by a hearing aid. There are many treatments and electronic devices available that do something as simple as increase the volume on a television set for one person. If your senior resists visiting an audiologist it may be necessary to let her know that this is not her decision alone. A hearing problem affects the whole family. It is imperative that a diagnosis be made. If there are different options so far as treatment, let her make the final decision.

Gerry was the lady who came to help with Nanny. But Nanny could tell by Gerry's body language that things weren't going well between them. It seemed that there were a lot of things that Gerry wouldn't talk about because she knew Nanny would not agree. Nanny, however, would rather have Gerry express how she felt. It would be much easier than seeing a look of disappointment or disapproval. When Gerry sighed at her, Nanny would try to do better. Often Nanny didn't know what she had done. She decided that Gerry was giving up on her when Gerry didn't talk much or busied herself in the other rooms. Nanny was afraid that

Gerry might quit. The answer to the problem is that Nanny and Gerry need to know that it's all right to express different opinions. It doesn't matter if you have different ideas, preferences or beliefs. The main thing is that we should respect another's right to express themselves. No one needs to win or please everyone all the time.

Mutual Respect—Not Maid Service

Jane's mother kept her very busy. "Jane, will you bring me some Kleenex?" Jane obeyed. A few minutes later her mother rang her little bell. Jane came immediately. "Jane, I need a box of my laxative tablets. Would you get them, now? It's only a little way to the drug store." Jane went and got her purse and said she'd be back soon.

When Jane came home her mother said, "It's really hot in here. Do we still have my fan in the basement? Could you bring it up?" Jane went to the basement and brought up the fan. It was heavy. John could have carried it much more easily but he wasn't home and Jane wanted her mother to be comfortable.

These requests went on all day long. It's not that they were unreasonable or difficult to perform. The problem is that they were constant. They broke into Jane's routine. She felt irritable and pressured. She loved her mother and was sorry that her mother couldn't do as much as she used to. But Jane made the mistake of putting herself in her mother's service so that now her mother expected it and was unaware of the inconvenience she was causing. Jane's mother believed that doing for others was a way of showing love. Jane knew this, and if she refused her mother would get very quiet and let Jane know that she was a very ungrateful daughter.

As a result, Jane felt like "running away." She began to avoid going in to her mother's room. When these requests occurred once too often Jane snapped at her mother and said, "I'm only one person, Mother." (When she would talk to her friends she would complain about how demanding her mother is.)

Jane could bring harmony back into their home if she would treat herself with respect. Blaming her mother will not help. They are both playing a part in a script that is continuously being acted out. Jane needs to extricate herself from this pattern of behavior. She must avoid getting angry by deciding what she is and is not willing to do. She could say, "I'm busy right now but we'll keep a list by your chair. I can do the things you need during a time of day that's convenient to both of us. She needs to be firm and friendly. No attack or resentment is necessary. Being firm and friendly, without dominating or getting back at someone, shows love and concern.

Avoiding Overprotection

Every evening at 7:00, Marie would go into her mother's room to get her mother ready for bed. Marie knew that her mother wanted to take care of herself but she was afraid something would happen. Marie thought her mother might slip and fall or get a chill if she didn't change her clothes fast enough. Marie was worried that her mother's teeth might get cavities if Marie didn't supervise the brushing. Marie saw danger lurking in every corner.

Marie's mother looks forward to the time when she can get ready for bed. It gives her something to do. She can decide whether she needs her flannel nightie or a more "summery" one. She can walk slowly into the bathroom and not worry about taking too long while Marie is standing there, waiting. She can brush her teeth and take time to see if they're clean. She can do her evening devotions and go over the day without interruption.

"I can't go so fast anymore," Mother says. "I wish Marie wouldn't be so afraid. Maybe she knows something about my health and isn't telling me. I feel good. I wish she'd let me do the things I can do."

When we overprotect our loved ones we discourage them. Often they feel helpless. If we don't show confidence in them, they often begin to think that they, too, should worry. If we do things for them that they are able to do for themselves, they often do less and less. When this happens, their bodies and minds don't get enough exercise and may become weaker and weaker. A more positive approach might be to say, "Here, Mother, you start your washing and if you need help just call or ring this little bell." Courage and confidence grows if we have faith in them.

We can stop being a shield to protect our seniors from life. Instead, we can become a filter that can stop and determine which acts our seniors are able to accomplish and which might be too difficult. We can ask and listen to what they say. If given the opportunity, they will know their limitations and share them with us. It is usually only when they feel restricted and controlled that they will attempt something which might endanger them. At that time they may be acting out of anger or rebelliousness rather than good sense.

Minding Our Own Business

Arthur's mother lives with Arthur and his wife Jean, who works part time. Arthur is away from 7:30 AM to 5:30 PM. When he gets home he usually flops in a chair and dozes until dinner time. This makes his mother very upset. She feels that he should treat her with respect and come in to see her as soon as he gets in the door. She tells Jean repeatedly that this is very important to her and that it makes her feel so sad and rejected that she wants to move away. "There, now, don't cry, Mother Jones, I'll talk to him. He doesn't realize how badly you feel." Jean says hoping to make things better.

Jean goes to the living room and tells Arthur to please go in and say "Hello" to his mother when he comes home. Arthur feels that he is doing enough, taking care of his mother. His two sisters have refused to do anything. "She should know that I care about her or I wouldn't be having her here," says Arthur. "She may think she can move away but where would she go?" Variations of this scenario are duplicated over and over again. In many instances the relative of the elderly person brings her into the home and then abdicates all responsibility for her care. Arguments ensue, tempers flare and the whole atmosphere of the home becomes a powder keg waiting to explode. Relationships between two people belong to those involved. Mother's relationship with Arthur belongs to them.

Jean has no obligation to control their interaction. She has a choice in what is most comfortable for her when she relates to Arthur's mother. If she tries to rescue Arthur's mother she will only intensify the situation. Mother will feel more and more helpless and unloved and Arthur will experience guilt and anger when Jean barges in. Jean's most effective action could be to reassure her mother-in-law and encourage her to talk to Arthur about her concerns. Jean's greatest strength could be to count to ten, remind herself that advising and giving solutions are not ways to strengthen Arthur's mother. It is always helpful to offer to help someone explore different avenues they can take, but make sure this is what they want. Jean might say, "What would happen if you did this?"

When Your Elderly Loved One Seems Unhappy

Jim's Uncle Roy seemed to be so quiet and sometimes Jim noticed that Uncle Roy had tears in his eyes. Jim knew he didn't act the same as he did before the operation. It was hard for Uncle Roy to get around now. He said he didn't want to bother anyone, "I don't know why God is keeping me around." The doctor didn't want to put Roy on anti-depressant drugs because of side effects. So Jim decided to take a week off and work on the problem. He decided to "take the bull by the horns" and talk to Uncle Roy. Jim suggested that they explore what could be done to make life happier. Jim would listen, make a list and help Uncle Roy try one thing at a time. Jim knew that there were buses that came into the neighborhood to take seniors to the center. Uncle Roy liked to play cards and sing. Neither of these things would be hampered by his inability to walk very well.

Jim knew that Uncle Roy was lonely for his wife who had died during the winter. Roy would talk about how she was so much better off, since she had been in so much pain. But he would never talk about his feelings. Jim decided that along with planning some group activities he would make a point of spending time with his uncle. He would sit with him, smile, pat him on the shoulder and even do some more intimate services such as helping him cut his toenails. Jim would try to find out what activities were difficult for Uncle Roy to accomplish. Then they could practice together new ways of working it out. ·

Jim knew that he had some habits, himself, that might hurt Uncle Roy's feelings. He talked loud and fast and expected his uncle to answer immediately. He didn't have trouble talking to his uncle but Jim wasn't a very good listener. That was something Jim could change.

One night Jim came home later than usual. He could see panic in his uncle's eyes. That night he talked to him about his fears and what they might do about them. If the fears were real Jim could help Uncle Roy work out a plan. Jim would call if he were going to be late so Roy could check the door locks. If they were imagined he could encourage Uncle Roy by showing confidence in his ability to cope and let him know how courageous he had been throughout the past year. These seemingly "little things" helped Roy bounce back to his "old self" and put a smile back on his face.

Fear

Fear is such a complicated emotion. We can be afraid of being alone. We can fear being hurt. We sometimes fear rejection. Humiliation scares us. Having no feeling of belonging is a scary thing. All these fears seem to be intensified as we grow older and experience a decrease in our competence.

When I was recovering from my brain operation I noticed that my memory was not as sharp as it had been before I was ill. All kinds of thoughts raced through my head. Was it because part of my brain had died? Was it because I was "getting old?" Was I in the first stage of Alzheimer's? One thing was sure. I was afraid. It was then I learned how debilitating fear can be. I began to use it to excuse me from performing. I found that it gave me attention and sympathy. It gave me power to have others think for me and serve me. As time went on I realized that I was beginning to feel important for many reasons, all based on my perceived inadequacy. As this behavior continued, it grew, and I didn't like who I was becoming. It was right about that time that I read *Love is Letting Go of Fear* by Gerald Jampolsky. I think if I were to re-title that book I would name it "Love Drives Out Fear" because I found that the only way for me to feel confident and courageous again was to show love to any person or in any situation when I was fearful. The two can't exist together. Loving takes the place of fear. You can only do one at a time and the positive one, love, always wins.

If the person you're caring for is fearful it's usually a call for love. What's going on in her life that leads her toward this feeling of discouragement? When she says, "You never spend any time with me" is she really saying, "I'm afraid you don't love me any more?" When she says, "Don't go out, I'm feeling sick this morning," is she telling you she's afraid to be alone? If you hear, "You hate me," does she mean "I'm afraid I'm too much trouble and no one will like me?" When she says, "Let me alone" is she saying she's given up and feels hopeless? Whatever she's saying, a moment of encouragement and loving can begin to heal the pain in her heart. Fear cannot stay when love is present.

Dealing With Difference Of Opinion

No two persons feel the same way about everything. One person's way is never the "only" way. In many instances, right and wrong are only a matter of perception and are conclusions made from individual past experience. If we wish to have our relationship one of impartiality, honesty, and equality we must be willing to reevaluate our thinking. If I make a dogmatic statement to my daughter about Johnny's clothing being too casual for school, it would help if she acknowledged the fact that we have different viewpoints. She might say something like, "You may be right. I'll think about it." If the discussion has to do with our relationship, we could bring it up later and explore ways to compromise or accept differences. If it has the added facet of being Johnny's problem, we may need to recognize together that it is his choice and his responsibility to experience the consequences of his behavior.

When we all gathered for dinner there were four generations, each having something to say after a day of being apart. Often each member spoke from an entirely different frame of reference and the talk got louder and more lively. You could almost predict the moment when Nana would come in with, "Let's change the subject," or "Oh, dear, let's not argue." Having been brought up in an era when you never questioned your parents and a challenge to any older member was a mark of disrespect, Nana feared any hint of what she interpreted as a disagreement.

Differences of opinion don't have to be frightening. If they get loud, it is usually because someone is feeling threatened or in a losing position. When this happens, we often feel all the more determined to prove we are right. If this is not possible, we may go on to attack the person whom we feel has defeated us.

Marlo Thomas talked and sang about being "Free to be You and Me." Is anything we say to one another so important that it can wield the power to affect our feeling of worth? We can always consider the source and the statement and then come to our own conclusion about its significance in our life.

Expressing Pity Doesn't Help

Bill's grandmother wanted to attend his wedding. She had waited so long for him to find a nice girl and "settle down." Now that the day was almost here she realized that she wouldn't be able to go. Her strength was failing and she was confined to her bed. She cried and cried. "It isn't fair," she sobbed

"I know, Grandma" said Bill. "We'll have a tape made of the wedding and we'll stop by and see you on the way to the reception."

"You don't understand," Grandma wailed. "It isn't the same. I got a new dress and everything. I want to go."

Bill grew more and more upset. "I'm sorry that it's such a terrible disappointment. It's such a shame that it turned out this way. Life is so hard for you."

Bill thought he was being kind and understanding but actually he was reinforcing Grandma's belief that she is a person to be pitied. By saying to Grandma that she has such a horrible life he helps her become convinced that the world owes her much more, even though she has had a very meaningful life.

This may have been prevented in part, by preparing Grandma for a possible disappointment. Another way to encourage her would be to show confidence that she would be able to handle her disappointment and get enjoyment from the tape and visit Bill had mentioned.

Giving Grandma the belief that she should never be thwarted in any plan she has made only strengthens the idea that she is special and should experience only success. This is not possible. It's never too late to learn that life is full of ups and downs.

Giving Strokes For Self-Esteem

Many of the mistakes we make in child-rearing are the same ones we make with our seniors. Have you ever noticed that children like to help around the house when they are little but quickly become turned off or disinterested? I think it's for the same reasons that our seniors begin to isolate themselves and refrain from offering help. We think we can do it faster. We think we can do it a better way. It's often easier to do the work alone. Often we think we are being kind and loving by doing it "for" them.

We say things like "let me do that, you're too shaky," or "I'll do it, you're too slow." It's not only what we say. It's how we say it. It's our tone of voice, the look on our face and our "body language." We let them know we doubt their ability to accomplish a task. We must separate the "deed from the doer." We need to let them know that their action does not affect their value as a person.

When Nana decided to learn to crochet, she was 80 years old. She soon found that it was difficult and became discouraged. Thank goodness, her granddaughter was there to say, "That's okay, try again. It'll get easier and then you'll have fun doing it."

Comparing is another way we discourage. It doesn't matter how old you are, it hurts to hear, "How come you can't balance you checkbook? Aunt Mary always could and she was older than you are!"

Another mistake we often make is expecting the senior to make a mistake and saying something that sends that message. "Oh, Mother, don't try to pour the milk on your cereal, you'll probably spill it."

Dr. Dreikurs said we all need *The Courage to be Imperfect* (the title of his biography by Pew and Turner). To maintain this courage it really helps for a senior to have someone give words of encouragement. These words must be words that convey a confidence in the person. They say, "I have faith in you. I believe that you can do it." They are said at any time. They are not just words of praise after an accomplishment. They say, "You're an okay person, whether you succeed or fail at a task."

Rewards Don't Work

"Come on Aunty, finish your dinner and I'll give you some candy." What does this say to Aunty? "I really don't care about what you want for dinner, or how you're feeling. How you act depends on my power over you. You don't have any right to decide for yourself. You can't control what you eat. I know what is best for you. I'm the authority here."

Promising a reward for doing something that is her own responsibility is a way to teach Aunty that it's only necessary to act when she's going to get a reward. The action is not based on her need for food, rest, medicine or exercise. It is based on another person's power. It is based on "What will I get?" rather than, "What would be good for me?" It puts the caregiver in a superior position and the senior in an inferior one. It is often manipulation and deception.

Statements such as, "The doctor says this may improve your breathing," or, "This may give you more energy," are facts that give information. They are statements shared by equals. Sharing information is a mark of respect. Bribery is an insult to the senior's dignity and intelligence.

Promising rewards often has an element of dishonesty associated with it. We think we will make an experience easier to bear but it may come out just the opposite. Let's say there's a 50-50 chance that a hip operation will correct a problem. We want our senior to have it and think it will help. Then we say, "You'll be able to walk just like you used to." We are setting her up for a terrible disappointment if it doesn't do the job. The truth, no matter how hard to face, is a more loving approach than glossing over the situation. As long as she is capable of deciding (even if it is not the decision you would make), she deserves the consideration and esteem given when she has the opportunity to think about a choice and decide upon a course of action.

Consequences

Adele's mother was at the stage when she could not remember when to take her medicine. She had some close calls when she took too much medicine too close in time. This was a matter of health. Adele decided to take action. She either administered the medicine herself or designated someone else to do it. Although Mother was hurt and angry, this was for her own good.

George's father would not stay in bed at night. He would roam in the dark. George purchased bed rails. His father persisted, and climbed over the rails and fell, cutting his head. Then George gave his father a choice. He could stop climbing out or be tied in bed at night. (When consequences are discussed no threats should ever be made if you are not willing to carry them out. A short explanation can be given of the need for safety. You must be sure of your plan and not willing to enter into arguments).

Martha had spoken to her dad about not driving anymore. Even though he had some near misses, and his judgment was failing, he was determined to hang onto his car. Martha decided that the time had come to act. She would tell him that she was not willing to ride with him anymore because she believed it was unsafe. If this would not influence him she was ready to contact the Motor Vehicle Bureau and ask them if they would be willing to have him tested to determine whether he was competent to handle a vehicle. Fortunately, the latter action was not needed. Martha's father realized that if Martha refused to ride with him it must be time to stop driving. It hurt her dad's pride, but that was better than having someone hurt or killed in an accident.

Aunt Catherine was having trouble knowing when she needed to go to the bathroom. It embarrassed her. But, she couldn't talk to her niece and nephew about it. She thought they might suspect—sometimes her clothes got damp. What could she do? Aunt Catherine's niece knew how private Aunt Catherine was about personal things, so she asked Aunt Catherine if she would mind seeing her doctor for a checkup just to make sure everything was all right. Aunt Catherine breathed a sigh of relief and said, "Yes." The doctor was able to make a diagnosis and recommend the right procedure. When privacy is involved we must treat the senior with dignity, but we also must take care of the problem. Sometimes it is helpful to ask ourselves, "How would I want to be treated in this situation?"

If the senior that you care for has developed a very difficult personality, and constantly criticizes you, there must be a consequense for this behavior. Sometimes Emma would be nasty to her daughter and at other times not speak at all. It really hurt Betsy. She tried hard to keep her mother happy. This may have been part of the problem. We can't make others happy. Betsy would leave her mother's room a confused, angry, sad young woman. Often she would be crying. She decided to talk to a counselor about it because it was affecting her marriage. Betsy was advised to continue to visit but when her mother was negative she should say, "It seems that you don't feel like talking now. I am going to go do my studying. I'll be back and visit again later." Betsy was advised not to argue or appease or mollify her mother. Just leave, but always give another chance. As a result her mother became more friendly.

The consequence of doing everything for your senior encourages them to become dependent. Older persons already have lost some of their confidence. Often we do things for them because we are in a hurry and know we can get things done much faster. Other times we serve them because we believe it's a way to show love. How would you feel if someone came into your room and grabbed your clothes out of the closet and put them on you?

One day I was visiting in a nursing home and a woman volunteer walked up to a person in a wheel chair. The volunteer pushed her into the solarium saying, "See how nice it is in here. Look at the sunshine. Here are all your friends." The occupant of the wheel chair had a surprised look on her face. "I wonder who this is?" When the volunteer finally "parked" her and went on to someone else I heard the resident say, "But I just came from here, I was on my way to my room!" It's important for us to ask before we "rescue" someone. Being independent is a goal of most humans.

Guilt Feelings

Whenever we talk about changing our behavior in our "Caregivers" group it is inevitable that the following comment will come up: "Oh, I can't do that, I would feel so guilty!"

Guilt feelings are a symptom and have a purpose. They can best be understood if the purpose is understood. The main significance of guilt feelings lies in the service they provide to the individual who is striving toward a goal. In contrast to actual guilt (I did it, or I didn't do it), guilt feelings are subjective perceptions.

Sometimes one will express guilt feelings to prove their worth. This is a sign of good intentions. When they have done something they believe is wrong, feeling guilty about the behavior is a way to salve their conscience.

When an individual feels inadequate they may use guilt feelings to compensate by getting others to feel sorry for them. "If I let others know how hard I tried and how guilty I feel about not reaching my goal, they will know how much I suffer, and see the nobility in me."

Guilt feelings are a way to have others excuse behavior. They may also induce others to change their behavior.

It is human to fall short, but this does not imply that guilt feelings must follow. Guilt feelings get in the way of effective actions that can lead to improved relationships. It is not necessary to feel guilty in order to feel good. To remove guilt feelings is to make room for confidence.

Part 4

Grandma's Loved Ones

Who Is The Grandpa I Know?

If I see my role in life as a channel of God's loving thoughts, creativity, and intelligence. If I am a vessel to pour these elements out to each being I touch during this earthly existence—then where does "Grandpa," my partner, my beloved, my helpmate, fit into this huge complicated picture?

He came into this world ready and willing to assume the role which God had given him. The lifestyle he chose, as his "road map," as early years of sincere searching for his place rolled by, was one of direct honesty, kindness, hard work and a ravenous appetite for knowledge.

How did we find each other, stay together, grow together into a healthy, holy relationship through good times and bad, the sweet and bitter, sorrow and joy? We started out by looking for someone to fill the deep caverns of emptiness within us. We had each come from relationships that had started full of hope and ended in pain.

The grandpa I know today weathered with strength, courage, understanding and healthy self-esteem the feminist movement which angered and baffled many fine men. He accepted my self-appointed role of all-knowing, single-handed child raiser, all the while realizing that somehow we were out of balance and needed more equal participation in our parenting.

When he found the answer to our dilemma, he threw himself into a new dedication to correct our mistaken belief that, "If you just do what your parents did the kids will come out all right." As a result of this new awareness, he has come to believe and live the principles of encouragement and love that he counsels and studies each day.

He is a living example that while one rarely changes his lifestyle he can change his behavior within it to find peace with his brothers and sisters of this world and live a better life.

When I was a young and foolish girl of 19, my only aim in life was to find someone who would fill the hole in my soul and make up for the lack I felt and the emptiness that engulfed me. So I found a handsome, good dancer, who vowed his eternal love. *Eternity* lasted three years. I think right then I began to realize that there were two kinds of relationships. The first one was the kind that made up for a perceived lack—finding a "special" person who would solve all my concerns—a Prince Charming. Then, there was in my second marriage a "Holy" relationship that was very different. God had sent me a lesson and an answer. My answer has lasted 43 years. The "Holy" relationship, as I see it, is one based on the principles of encouragement and love I've talked about before. It is working together, each partner accepting the other as she/he is, dealing with all concerns and crises with love and forgiveness. It's knowing that we rarely can change our lifestyle, but we can change our behavior within it to find peace and joy with our partner. It's knowing that there will always be problems but that we can with the guidance of the Holy Spirit, solve them.

How Have We Stayed Together For 43 Years?

I talked with my mother-in-law last night. She's 89 years-old and still going strong. It's so neat to be able to talk about almost anything. Yesterday she said, "If you ever do decide to write a book (and I think you should), there should be a part where you tell why you and Don have such a strong lasting relationship."

I said, "I'll try." But then I got to thinking, "That's a hard one! Having been a counselor for many years, it's a lot easier to diagnose other people's concerns and help them grow and change than it is to analyze your own."

Having had an unhappy first marriage, I knew what I wanted if I ever married again. We are asked in our counseling sessions, "What attracted you to your mate?" This seemed unimportant when we thought of the long commitment we both desired. Being cute, a good conversationalist or a great dancer suddenly plummeted to the bottom of our lists. Finding a balance between closeness and apartness was high. Putting our partner first, but also feeling free to do things independently, solidified our trust and love. Having similar interests was important, but not as important as respecting the fact that we might not have them.

When differences come up, searching for the real problem helps. So often we are tired and angry at the end of a work day and pounce on any little thing that has nothing to do with our real concern.

Don and I decided that we had to prioritize our problems and not "make mountains out of molehills." We've found that a short blowup sometimes clears the air and then we can go on without hours of sulking or silence.

A determination to make our marriage work, no matter what, not only helped us rate our concerns but made us work each day on improving our life together.

Patience makes for a calm, warm atmosphere. Humor lightens the heavy atmosphere. Assertiveness (a vow to work together as equals) brings respect to a partnership.

A tolerance for difference in personality can lead us to cooperation rather than having to determine who's right and who wins.

Friendship came first with us. It gradually bloomed into a loving team which matures each year. Acceptance and a tolerance for imperfections and mistakes are nurtured by encouragement. Realizing that the best way to heal a wound is to work on myself and understanding my part in the conflict works wonders.

Allegiance to the marriage first, and everyone and everything else second, brings joy. All you have to do is love and forgive. To love God, your partner, your fellow being, and yourself is our answer.

Let Me Tell You About My Grandchildren!

On Halloween morning in 1980, my daughter called from West Virginia. "The pains are 5 minutes apart, Mom. We're going to the birthing center." Since this was our first grandchild, my heart beat like a trip-hammer. I was scared, excited, and praying for a safe delivery and a healthy baby. I couldn't function. I spent most of the day on the hill in the side yard hugging Queenie, our German Shepherd, and waiting for the phone to ring. I repeatedly called John, the husband of my daughter's friend who had accompanied them to the center.

"No news yet," he'd say over and over. After 37 hours of waiting and fearing the worst, the news came. All was right with the world. We had a grandson.

On that same day my dad called from Florida to say that my mother had had a mastectomy. "Which way should I go?" To Florida to Mom or to West Virginia to my daughter. I did both. I found my mother in good spirits (at 82 years-old) and then went on to Pittsburgh and took the smallest plane I had ever seen over the fields and hills to Morgantown. At times I felt I could touch the grass. I sat only a few feet behind the pilot. As we landed, I saw my son-in-law's car pull up. I peeked into the car seat. There was a little "Eskimo" bundled up with only a little pug nose showing, even though it was a warm day for November first.

I had vowed to keep my nose out of their business and only act when asked, but we soon learned that this little one had a very strong mind of his own. He didn't want to nurse if it involved any work. He'd drink the sugar water supplement the hospital had advised but only because it was easy. On the fifth day of this little guy's life we had the first of our many "discussions." His mother was frantic with worry that he would die if he didn't eat soon. I said, "Jeff, you know this is a cooperative effort. Mom gives you the milk and you drink it. It makes both of you feel better. You're not getting any more sugar water." At that moment those gorgeous gray eyes looked up at me for the first of hundreds of subsequent times and focused right on mine. They as much as said, "Who are you? What part do you play in my life? Can I trust you?" I felt the arms of God engulfing us and a love that has lasted from that day to this. Being a mother fulfilled my fondest wish. Being a grandma has given me an undreamed of gift from God.

The second grandchild was just the opposite in her choice of how to come into this world. Her parents kept thinking, "It's going to get a lot worse" so they fixed their dinner and began to eat. Jessica had other ideas. They had a roller coaster ride to their hospital just making it in time for my second daughter to deliver her beautiful baby girl. My visit to help care for her was a joy. The baby's father and

I would respond to a request for a diaper change with a hearty shout of "Poop squad!"

Our third grandchild, Katharine, came to us for just a brief moment. She had a tumor in her heart and stayed only 7 days. I never got to meet her, and yet, I believe she changed the lives of our whole family in that short time. We learned how precious each minute of life is. We learned to put compassion for others before our own self-centered interests. We learned that a tiny spirit can influence the values, beliefs and faith of each one she touches. I am thankful each day for the love she created in our family.

Number four is a precious redhead with big chocolate-colored eyes and a smile that would melt a glacier. He loves everyone he meets and at two-years-old lets them know it by looking them straight in the eye and saying, "I like you!" And they like Rob.

Our next addition is a "white tornado." Kevin is a cuddle bunny who is interested in everything that exists in his world. Already, at 18 months, he has a fan club of multitudes.

Number six is a happy, peaceful, cooperative young "man." He went to the grocery store at one week old and to church at two weeks. Wesley just joined the family as if he'd always been there.

So, you see, I just had to tell you about my grandchildren. Many years ago, when I wasn't fortunate enough to have any I'd say, "I'm never going to be one of those grandmothers that drags out her pictures every time she meets someone." Ha! People do make mistakes, you know! On Father's Day, as I sat in the garden my younger son and his wife had created, overwhelmed by the blessings God had heaped on us, I felt the spirit of love and forgiveness that was alive in that group. I thought, over and over, "I have reached my goal." As an only child this was my quest: To feel self-confident and have a family who loves God and their sisters and brothers.

A Letter To My Grandson After An All-Star Baseball Game

Last night was a growing experience about life. How wonderfully you grew! You did your job in a most skillful manner and held your head high as a result.

This year has changed you from a little boy to a fine young man. It doesn't mean that there won't be problems. Everyone has them. But you now have the ability to cope with them with God's help.

There's no need for regret or disappointment when you know that Jesus always walks with you and strengthens you with wisdom, understanding, courage, and confidence. God gives you His unconditional love which you now pour out to those around you. When I saw you at the close of the game, walking tall, with a friendly smile while shaking hands with the opposing team, I thanked God for putting you in my life.

My Mother-In-Law

Atta called yesterday. She is such a dynamo. She is such a beautiful example of a child of God. Her life has been days ranging from jubilation to tribulation. Through all these days of her 80-plus years she has accepted God's challenge and now as her heart tells her it's tired and worn she stands at the door of a new chapter in her book of life. Tests of endurance, such as the death of her first husband, raising two grandchildren when her son was unable to do so, and weathering the cool reception given her by in-laws who found it hard to accept such a free spirit, have all fine-tuned this instrument of music, art and intellect.

To me, she is another example of a miracle. When she came into our lives after Don's mother's untimely death, I saw her as an invader, a usurper of her predecessor's rightful place, a thief who came to take away Don's father's love. How wrong I was! She turned a broken, crushed survivor into a man full of smiles and energy, eager to meet life again.

I said to Don this morning (with admiration), "She's a tough old bird!" She has so many qualities I'd like to have. She talks freely and honestly about her beliefs. She is ready to have her body die, but still has a few things she'd like to tidy up before she goes. While she waits, she'll take a plane to Michigan this summer to visit friends. What courage! What a joyful acceptance of life, whatever she is served.

I believe our relationship changed only after I looked at her in a new way. I accepted this new "actor in our play of life" as different but with interest and respect. I joined enthusiastically in her interests of painting, music, and jewelry-making. I understood the trials of her challenge of rearing two young children, starting when she was in her 50's. I let her know I believed she could do it. I replaced blame I had first felt with feelings and acts of love. I listened. I tried to practice the elements of encouragement.

Exchanging Roles With My Adult Children

When I was at my adult child's home recently a kind of revelation came over me. I am no longer the "sandwiched generation." My mother and father have both gone on. I am now the senior generation in our family. I am having feelings of confusion about my role. It is not frightening, but rather puzzling. I don't know whether what I'm doing is helping or just making things more complicated for my adult children. I don't know when they are doing things to give me a feeling of being needed or when they really want help. I guess the answer is to bring this out in the open and just ask. I understand my Mom and Dad so much more, now. I'm actually walking in their shoes. I feel I've made a step forward, though. I know that they understand.

Some examples of this new arrangement I find myself in: My adult child said not to come down early in the morning because it would be more confusing getting her kids off to school. I can remember feeling exactly the same way when my Mom got up early to help fix breakfast. So, I've learned. It works fine. I actually like to sleep a little longer—but even if I didn't, I could read or write and wait until things calmed down.

Another example: I start to do something to help, like make the beds. Then I think, "What if my daughter wants to change them today? What if I don't do them the way she does?" Just little things, but I can see much more clearly now.

At this stage of my thinking I have decided that my action will be based upon complete openness and honesty: no laying guilt trips on anyone, no sad looks, no quiet withdrawal, no resentment at feeling controlled. I will get busy doing something for myself to keep alert, enjoy life and grow. I will let my children know I am available to help when they ask but not be an extra concern for them to deal with.

Let's look at things from a different angle. What if I think I need help and my adult child doesn't offer it? I must first identify the problem.

1. Am I expecting too much service?
2. Am I expecting him to read my mind?

3. Do I forget what I need until it is an inconvenient time for him (or them)?
4. Do I underestimate the responsibilities she has?
5. Have I sorted out my desires into wishes, wants, or real needs?

Another discovery I have made recently is that when there is too much action going on around me, when there is noise, conflict, or a need to hurry, I become discouraged and weepy. I tire easily, don't think as clearly, and feel confused. When this happens I often tend to blame someone else. For instance, I blame my daughter (or son) for allowing the children to be too noisy. Isn't it interesting that I worked with little children for years and rarely noticed the noise? I must face the fact that it isn't them, it's me. Another circumstance: I blame my adult child for being impatient with me for my slowness. He or she is not the one who is impatient. I am. I expect to go as fast as I did when I was 30. I must accept change.

It's important to understand that each one of your adult children is unique. There may be qualities that you see from the very first that remind you of another member of the family. You may hear statements like, "Oh, that smile is just like Uncle Charlie's." The bottom line is that no two people are alike. It would be a dull, strange world if they were. One adult child may have a clean but cluttered "lived in" home that usually has something minor that needs repair. Another adult child may really enjoy keeping things orderly, fixing things, keeping his environment controlled and orderly. Neither is right or wrong, bad or good. The only one who could be wrong, if I disapprove or try to change their way of living, is me!

A Letter To My Daughter

I'm up with a "noseful" at 4 AM. Hay fever has struck again. So I thought I'd write. So many things I'd like to talk about. When you said, "I know it may not be easy," when you were contemplating a new relationship I realized how much you had learned and grown and become a beautiful flower of womanhood. It's the difference between the impulsiveness of someone plunging into a relationship out of longing for companionship, and the opposite behavior of knowing life for what it is, from living it and accepting its peaks and valleys. It's living with gratitude each glorious moment of the gifts of happiness you recognize. I see now that when you used to get really discouraged it was partly because I taught you early in life that life shouldn't have any pain. Well, I still believe it would be great if it didn't but that's not the way it is. You've come to a point where you have learned that, too, through living. You know how I always say that God sends us lessons. Perhaps, since you have had a really difficult life being a single parent God may now be saying, "See what love and courage and forgiving can do?" Whenever we feel discouraged and doubtful God sends a lesson of reassurance. It's a miracle that you have learned to combine unconditional love, self-esteem and wisdom at such a young age. Some, like Nana, wait 'til 92, some, like me, get flashes of it at 66, and some unfortunately never do.

When my Mom (unknowingly) would call me from work to put the pot roast on, then hang up without even saying, "Goodby," I vowed that whenever I could, I would always try to let my cherished ones know they were loved.

I love you,

Mom

Reminiscing

Last night I went to my "Caregivers" meeting on "Reminiscences." It was very interesting. The speaker from AARP told us how it helped seniors to reminisce. She explained that it helped them find peace and it even improved their physical, mental and emotional health. It's interesting that as we grow older we seem to remember happenings that occurred long ago much more easily than recent incidents. I certainly do. What does sharing these memories do for us? It gives us history that otherwise could be lost forever. It gives us pleasure when we share funny stories. I remember my mother telling a story that never ceased to make us laugh. When Mother was a little girl, and the family went on vacation, and it was time to wash the dishes (which was a job set aside for her and her cousin) the two children would always "have to" go to the "outhouse." Then, they didn't return until the dishes were done. Even at age 90, when she would remember this, Mom would get a certain look in her eyes and laugh and laugh.

What can we do for the person who is sharing a memory? Listen! It is a healing experience to be patient and give your undivided attention. It is also important to make sure this isn't something that they wish to be kept confidential. This provides a feeling of closeness. It gives them a feeling of worth to share what they've done, and lets them know that they are important.

Tonight I talked to my daughter in Atlanta. She told me about her daughter, (age 8) who had just participated in her first horse show. She said, "Mom, she sits so straight in the saddle until she starts "posting;" then she clings to the horse's mane."

I said, "Well, maybe we shouldn't tell her about what happened to me when I was her age. The first time I rode a pony around a ring by myself the saddle came loose and I found myself hanging upside down under the pony's chubby little belly." We laughed and laughed. My daughter's husband always teases us about getting hysterical, but it sure is therapeutic for both of us. Once we get started it's hard to stop. Then we remember a time when we were getting gas for our little Volkswagen and I dropped the credit card next to me. I didn't realize that the attendant was waiting by the car window. I opened the door to get the card and we heard an "oouff!" I had smacked him right in a very sensitive area.

By the time we go through a few of these memories we have almost forgotten how much we miss each other. We've replaced the discouragement that comes from thinking of all the concerns of the world. We've lit our "one little candle" by bringing joy to a loved one. Reminiscence is the best medicine.

Puzzle Pieces That Make Up My Mind

My first dog, Rascal, was a black and shiny Cocker Spaniel. She always brought a potato out of the bin to visitors when they came to the door of our apartment. She was so happy to greet them that once she pittled a tiny pool on the kitchen floor and her tail spun like a propeller. I loved her. When we went to pick her out, the owner of the mother dog said, "I'm so sorry, she's the only one left. The other pups were tan so the mother didn't understand why Rascal was black. The mother dog thought the others would hurt the black pup so she killed them." At five years of age that was my first experience with how tragedy can come from misunderstanding. Rascal and Ann, two "only children" were inseparable for the next 13 years.

He loved her beauty, her intellect, her wit. She hurt him deeply. He said, "If I love her enough, things will change." After ten years, things didn't change. He went on with his life alone. He mourned the loss and then found bliss in his new life.

My friend was full of fun, life and talent. We often watched in amazement as she shared her brilliant ideas, wrote plays, gave talks, and counseled anyone who came to her in pain. Then one day a car ran a stop light, and we lost her. God greeted her in her caftans, green slicker coat, and her beautiful red hair.

He had to make sure she was the right one and it was time to marry. I stewed and fumed. She said, "That's OK I'll wait." Now they've been married five years and are as happy as can be. Patience.

My "flower child" went braless, never shaved her legs and marched on Washington as I prayed for her safety. Now, she's all I'd ever dreamed she'd be as I waited for her to be born in 1951.

Mabel was my "ideal." I used to go visit her on her farm each summer. While my parents molded me into their image of perfection, Mabel accepted me just as I was. One day I asked her, "How come you never get upset when I do something you don't agree with?"

She looked at me with a twinkle in her eye and a broad grin. "Everyone to their own opinion, said the old lady as she kissed the cow!"

My grandfather, 80 years-old, with two amputations from a railroad accident, always wanted to see us. We'd go 200 miles to get him, then bring him to our house and help him settle in. After a few minutes, he'd sigh, "Well, I've been here and had a good time. Now I guess it's time to go."

My friends would always tease me. "You think your dad is God and Don's Jesus Christ." Then I would sit back, smile mysteriously and say smugly, "Pretty close."

She left her beautiful Collie with her in-laws when she went on a trip. Katie, the loyal, trusting, and devoted friend was killed by a car while they were gone. "I will never forget her. I will never get over it," she said.

"I have to be alone," he said. Then he went to live with her. He left his infant son and wife. It took me years to forgive. But I did. It was just the wrong time, the wrong combination. However, he's proven over and over that he is a devoted father.

When Daddy died, Mom was furious. She thought he'd been faking his pain, as she sometimes did. Years later she cried when they turned her in her bed and she said, "Now I understand."

Part 5

Talking With God

A Memory Of Faith

It was a cold and snowy New Year's Eve. We were all visiting Nana and Bompa, (my parents). The children had played "store" and "restaurant" all day at the built-in bar in the basement. They loved the place. Although it was near the corner where a large highway passed, it was safely fenced. There were places to ride down a gentle slope in the back yard in an old baby buggy. In the back bedroom there was room for two twin beds and two cots. The children delighted in playing "throw the dirty sock" after the lights were out, until I would come storming down the hall waving my sneaker and yelling, "That's enough!"

But this night was different. After dinner we let Lady, our beautiful collie-shepherd, go outside. A few minutes later we called to her to come in. She didn't come. Everyone spilled out of the back door in various stages of undress. The kids were going to bed and Don and I were getting ready to go to a party. Nana and Bompa were to be the "sitters." After what seemed like a lifetime we came in. I started getting the children into bed and Don went out in the car to look for Lady. There were no sock fights that night. Everyone was in tears.

"Where is she? How did she get out? Will she come back? When?" All questions that I couldn't answer. I was beside myself with fear. I sat on the floor desperate for the answers and then it came to me. "I know what we can do! We can all pray that Lady will be safe and come home to us." Silence lay on the room like a soft comforter. After a few minutes the front door opened. Don came in, with Lady.

Amid the howls of delight from the four children and their tail-wagging, face-licking beloved friend, Don gave part of the answers to the questions we had asked. (Some we'll never know.) Lady, who had been frightened by another dog, had somehow gotten through a rail gate of the fence and had begun to wander. Don found her across the big highway, sitting on the porch of a house. Now, thirty-some years later, one of the children (who now have children of their own) will ask, "Remember the night that Lady was lost and we all prayed?"

Is There Life After Death?

I was so angry with God for allowing Mother to go on suffering. I was angry that I couldn't talk with her and know she heard. I was angry that she was afraid and alone. I was angry that she was in pain. I would never have believed that such a cruel thing could happen to such a fine woman. I felt half alive—like I was in a fog. I prayed so long for her to have peace. I felt so helpless. I was afraid we'd run out of money and then what would we do? Sometimes I felt like I was in the middle of a huge hoax. Sometimes I thought that I just made up a god and it was all a fantasy. I was so sure that I was on the right road. Then I wasn't sure. I had been loving and forgiving to all the people in my life. I couldn't forgive God. I was back in the old pattern of expecting certain things to happen if I did certain things. Without even knowing it, I was trying to make bargains with Him. Communicating with the Lord is not just another version of "Let's Make A Deal." You trust Him and give your life over to Him. Then you wait, no matter how long it takes. You learn that the crossing over of the spirit from here to eternity comes at the right time.

Spiritual Signals

There are two signals in my life that recur constantly. Each time I feel any negative emotion I believe it is a signal. This signal is a warning that goes off like an alarm system. It is telling me that something is not going as it should. It says, "Heads up, wake up, be alert, be aware!" It says, "Your perception is off the track and you're not seeing things as you should."

Whenever anything that I perceive as wrong or unfair happens to me or someone I love, my signal goes off. Sometimes the situation is well camouflaged to make it appear to be someone or something else in life that is to blame. I must be aware of this trickery my ego plays on me.

I believe that this signal is sent by God. It tells me to change my perception and to ask for help from the Holy Spirit. I believe God is letting me know what my next lesson is. If I need to grow spiritually in a certain area, God sends a situation and lets me know that it is my next assignment. My assignment is not to change others. It is not to project blame and use this skewed reasoning to avoid responsibility for my spiritual growth. Once I take the step of being aware of the signal I must then begin to deal with my perception.

Let's look at an example. My grandson does his homework. I look at it. It was done in a hurry and I think it's sloppy work. I feel angry. That's my signal. God is saying I still need to work on something. Then I have to figure out what it is. In this case it may be one of a number of things: Accepting others just as they are; pointing out strengths; minding my own business; or allowing differences of opinion. The most important lesson to work on is my spiritual growth with an attitude of loving and forgiving.

Once I get the signal, I must first decide if I sincerely wish to work on my spiritual growth. Second, if I do, I need to immediately ask for help from the Holy Spirit. Third, I must have loving and forgiving foremost in my mind as I work on changing my perception.

I mentioned earlier that there were two signals. The second one is even more exciting and miraculous than the first. If I have honestly and sincerely worked on my spiritual growth I will get the second signal. It may be in the form of an action or an actual change in my life. It may be an indication that the love and forgiveness I have sent has been received and is being sent back to me. It may be just a feeling of peace. In the example I mentioned about my grandson's homework, nothing was actually said. I had decided to send thoughts of love and acceptance. My second signal was his decision to do his paper over. Love was present. There was no room for anger. Love and anger cannot exist together.

Is Life Fair?

My teacher had a favorite saying that brought a chuckle to some people and infuriated others. It was, "Whoever said life was supposed to be fair?" Although I agree with this hypothetical query, I have found over the years that it's certainly not an empathic response to the human complaint of, "That's not fair." But is it a statement that needs consideration?

In all my years of life I have yet to meet anyone whose life has been "fair." This sample of research I present does not come only from clients I've treated in counseling. It also comes from my family, friends and others.

What is fairness? And who said that life should be fair? The dictionary says "fair" means: just, equitable, impartial, unbiased, dispassionate, objective. So, can life be "fair?" We are all human beings with a free will to choose what to think, believe, and do in the situations God presents to us. The

Bible says, "rejoice and be glad for great is your reward in heaven."

I believe that "fairness," or my reward, comes in the peace and joy I feel during and after any thought or act of love I experience. It can be in giving or receiving love or forgiveness. It can be tiny or large.

Those who think bad thoughts or do things which hurt themselves or others are crying out for love. They have not found the supportive loving friend who is the Holy Spirit. They have not yet learned that loving and forgiving is the only way. Fairness to one is not fairness to another. These conclusions are based on the illusions we create in our perception of life and our judgment of it. God said, "Judge not." An old Indian saying is "Judge not until you walk a mile in that person's moccasins." Life is life. To me it is my opportunity to learn and grow if and when I'm ready. I have a choice. I can stay with the hurt. I can fight or I can respond to it with love and forgiveness. Only the third choice will bring peace and obliterate the need to determine "fairness."

"I Could Have Called On God"

Remember the ad on TV when a man finishes a drink of soda with a very dull expression on his face? He then sees another person drinking and his face lights up as he shouts, "Wow, I could have had a V-8!"

A lady in our group was describing how she had been dealing with her problems in the same old discouraging way. Then, one day she realized that when she stopped to ask for help from God it gave her the strength and wisdom to find a solution. She said it was like, "Wow, I could have had a V-8!!" We all talked about this and said maybe the motto of our group could be, "Wow, I could have called on God!"

I've thought of this many times since she said it. She was at the stage in her life when she became aware of her hidden strength, God. Earlier in her life she had relied on only herself to act in a difficult situation, when all along she could have had God's help—if only she had asked.

Why don't we ask? Are we afraid that God won't come into our mind and heart and help us? Are we so steeped in the belief that if past experiences support our beliefs then that's the only way to go? These early conclusions are so strong they block off the only real, never failing, ever present loving Lord who can give us strength to cope with any exigency which may present itself.

Jane was raped when she was a child. As a result of that experience, she concluded that she could never trust anyone or anything other than herself. Now she has learned that even though her emotional wound still forms a wall at each step of her growth, every time she calls on the Lord for help He comes to her aid.

Marie decided long ago that she was of no value unless she obeyed her mother. Now, while caring for her dying mother, when Marie is stressed to the limit she cannot give the situation to God and find an alternative to her pain. I pray Marie will not wait too long to say, "I could have had God's help."

Pat was alone during much of her childhood. Her life was empty and she had no one to depend on. Now, in her 50's she has a hard time believing she can work together with her husband who, as part of God's plan, has been given to her after years of loneliness.

Letting go and letting God means just that. We need do nothing except follow the teachings of Jesus who said, in Matthew 7:7 *Ask, and it shall be given you; seek, and ye shall find; knock, and it shall be opened unto you.* We must say, "Please help me, God, to cope with this problem." The sooner we find this answer, the less likely we will be to ever have to say, "I could have called on God."

Why Is Praying So Hard?

One night at my "Caregivers" group many of us noted how embarrassed we felt that we didn't know how to pray. So, I decided to prepare a handout on communication with God that might help others and myself feel more comfortable when we needed to talk. I went on to enumerate the

How, When, Where and What of this communication. "How can I communicate with God?":

♥ With *Faith* that I am surrounded by God's love.

♥ With *Recognition* that the hardships and heartaches of life are lessons in my spiritual growth.

♥ With *Realization* that the unexpected is the norm and change is inevitable.

♥ With *Confidence* in others' ability to grow and in a peaceful outcome.

♥ With *Empathy* and *Understanding* of others.

♥ With *Love, Patience*, and *Forgiveness* rather than anger, blame or judgment.

♥ With the *Knowledge* that our expectations are never carried out exactly the way we want them to be no matter how hard we try to control them.

♥ With *Thanksgiving* for the blessings we have experienced.

♥ With a *Willingness* to listen to the "still small voice within" and to repel my doubts and change my perceptions.

♥ By *Taking* an active part in asking, seeking and knocking.

♥ By *Asking* God *"What would you have me do?"*

♥ By *Asking* God to guide my loved ones.

When Can I Communicate with God?

At any time during the night or day. For as little or long a time as I wish. No matter how I feel God is there welcoming me.

Where Can I Communicate with God?

In the church, on a crowded street or in my lonely room. It makes no difference, God can hear me.

What Shall I Talk About When I Communicate?

Anything that gives me pain, joy, confusion. Nothing is forbidden. God is always there for me.

Passing The Light

I always thought that psychology was one way to help people have better interpersonal relationships and religion was another way and "never the twain shall meet." I thought one had to choose. You'd think that someone who was a counselor for years would realize that in her own life there's always another way to look at a situation. Not so! I had to have a "revelation." This astonishing disclosure had to come after years of answered prayers and hundreds of hours of cognitive training.

Yesterday my friend told me about an experience she had driving on an icy road. She shared what she had learned as she saw this experience as a lesson from God. I realized that there was an entirely different lesson for me, in listening to her. She had learned about the kindness of strangers. I learned about my need for humility when I have a morally superior attitude and think, "I would never have gone out on a night like that."

Scripture tells us that we are the light of the world. We are to pass the light of Christ on to others. There is just one difference between being a messenger of God and one who just carries a message from place to place. It is receiving, then giving. This book is written so that I may remember the lessons God has taught to me. They have helped me grow. I'm sharing them with you but I don't expect you to get the same lesson as I.

When I was a child in Rochester, New York, we went to a small Methodist Church. I can remember sitting in the back row drawing on my bulletin. Every once in a while I would look up to see two pictures that hung on the walls before me. On one side was a stern old man seemingly coming out of the clouds with his arms raised toward me. This someone told me, was God. On the other side was a younger man with kind eyes and a beard, about to knock on a door. This, they said, was Jesus. Then, as the minister spoke he would often say, "God is Love" and Jesus and God were the same. We learned Bible verses. One was Mark 12:31 *You shall love you neighbor as yourself.*(NRSV) During the same period at home I was told "Don't think about yourself, you'll get a big head."

After many years of confusion and contemplation, I realized that I will never really know the whole truth while I'm in this earthly body.

In I John, Chapter 4, verse 16b, John writes, *God is love, and those who abide in love abide in God, and God abides in them.*(NRSV) Paul's letter in I Corinthians, Chapter 13, verses 4–8a says, *Love is patient; love is kind; love is not envious or boastful or arrogant or rude. It does not insist on its own way; it is not irritable or resentful; it does not rejoice in wrongdoing, but rejoices in the truth. It bears all things, believes all things, hopes all things, endures all things. Love never ends.*(NRSV) Paul is saying to me, "Love is the way and God is love."

During the past few years my family went through some very difficult times. They culminated in the near-death experience I had when, I believe, God said to me, "Don't you see, Ann, that it's so simple. All you have to do is love and forgive." It was at that time that I found what I call the "missing link." This was when the congruence of my spiritual walk and my psychological training became obvious to me. It was no longer possible for me to think of God and my training as separate. In counseling others I could use the tools and techniques of psychology but to make the therapy work I would have to add the "missing link." Recognizing a mistaken perception and correcting it was only half the battle. Just as important, was asking for guidance from God in an atmosphere of loving and forgiving myself and others.

"The light" is Christ, who is the light of the world. Jesus tells us in Matthew 22:37(NRSV) that the greatest commandment is, *...love the Lord your God with all your heart, and with all your soul, and with all your mind.* Doesn't this mean to love love? To put love first, honor love, respect love? Doesn't it mean to put love first in any situation?

Doesn't it mean to use love in your thoughts, words and actions in any situation? Doesn't it mean to see any happening whether negative or positive, as a cry for love?

What if, whenever we had a problem we would say, "Lord, please help me cope, with love. Not *my* will, but Thine be done."

Give Me The Courage To Face My Fears

I stood on the side of the boat and looked at the water ten feet below. The young man who was in charge of the snorkeling boat asked, "Do you want to jump or go off the ladder in the back?" (The other two times I had done this I had inched in from the back of the boat and received splinters in my backside and tears in my bathing suit.) This time was different. I had courage. It's hard to explain. I didn't consciously pray or think that God would take care of me. I knew. I knew if I wasn't foolhardy or impulsively careless there would be "no problem" as they say in the West Indies. I would be in God's arms. I jumped, and it was exhilarating! I had a feeling of going from one part of God's world into another. The warm cove waters caressed my body. I was surrounded by God's sea creatures. Tiny fry came in huge schools to welcome me to their home. The coral waved graceful arms to me as a welcome. Brightly-colored fish came up to my mask to study what this new specimen was that had invaded their territory. As I lay on top of the water, breathing calmly through my mouthpiece, a divine feeling of oneness with all living creatures came over me.

A few years ago, when we were snorkeling, we came upon a small shark lying on the bottom of the cove observing the swimmers. When we came back to the boat we asked, "Do you know there's a shark down there?"

The captain said, "Oh, pay no attention to him. He comes out every day. He just likes to look at the people!" How sad it is that we get such exaggerated ideas about other living species. We see "Jaws" and we conclude that all sharks are dangerous and should be destroyed. I remember holding a boa constrictor when I was teaching in Headstart and hearing its owner say, "Feel how warm and smooth she is? Don't worry, she's probably a lot more afraid of you than you are of her." Sensational books, movies and TV programs have taught us to be afraid of so many living things. I'd rather follow James Herriot's philosophy, "All creatures great and small . . . the lord God made them all."

I remember a prayer my mother taught me when I was very young. It ended with, "God is my all, I know no fear, since God, Life, Truth, and Love are here."

When A Body Dies

I feel strongly about giving dignity and respect to anyone whose spirit is about to leave their body. I want to do all

I can to give them support. I am not talking about helping someone rush the process. That's a whole other question that I haven't yet pondered. I believe in *living* wills. Both my husband and I have decided to have one. We do not want heroic measures when the time comes. I want to let my loved ones know that death does not have to be looked upon as something terrifying. I also want to let them know that I can go in peace because they have given me their love.

I believe that a person may have a lingering death for many reasons. When a person is taking a long time to die it may be because of some unfinished business that they may not know how to deal with. It could be that they are afraid that the ones left behind won't be able to cope with the change. It could be that they are so ill that they don't have the conscious ability to let go of life.

Often in attempting to be kind, caregivers may give false hope and tell the patient that they're getting better. This makes it more difficult for the patient. Medical professionals, in their need to heal, sometimes prolong the discomfort by forcing food and medicine past the point of no return.

My spirit will stay in this world as long as God permits it. My spirit will know when the time comes for it to leave this earth. In the meantime, it can use this earth as its classroom to grow in the love and forgiveness of our Lord.

What Is My Pain Saying To Me?

When I was a little girl Mom and Dad were very busy with community service, their social lives, and their work. As time unfolded, I discovered that the only way I could get much attention was to be sick. Many of my early memories of closeness with my parents are centered on when I had the measles, when I had my tonsils removed, and when I flew over the handlebars of my bike and had a concussion. As the years went by my subconscious mind told me, "When things get tough, get sick!"

As I grew older and learned about psychosomatic illness amazing things happened. If I were leading a group of about 100 Girl Scouts in a songfest I'd develop horrible stomach cramps. If I were counseling a difficult case in a family education center before an audience, I'd break out in scarlet hives. When the overload of work in my job as director of a Headstart program became unbearable, I developed Mononucleosis. By now, I was convinced that my "Illnesses" had a purpose. Sometimes I wasn't sure what. I explored many of the possibilities. They could be used to excuse me from failure, because I was convinced that I must do everything perfectly. They might be to let me get a rest when I had taken on way too many activities at once. They could be to get attention and sympathy from my family (as I had done in my childhood). I could often figure it out.

Last week was an example. We were getting ready to go to Atlanta to visit our daughter's family. I got a stiff neck and aching shoulders that would "choke a horse." What was my purpose? I certainly didn't want to get out of the trip I had planned for months. Then it came to me. What happens to me is not necessarily my planning. It can be the result of a poor decision I've made. For instance, I had been lugging around pieces of wood, logs from a tree that Don had cut down. At my age and with my arthritis, that was pretty stupid. There was something else that came to me as I stood in the shower with the hot water pouring on my neck. Couldn't this be another lesson from God? The more I thought, the more it all seemed to make sense. Wasn't He saying to me, "Let's be a little more humble. You don't have to be such a know-it-all. I have the truth." Maybe I was too smug about believing that I could heal myself. From now on I will check to see if my ego is speaking or if I am truly trying to live by God's Word.

Feeling Blue—What'll I Do?

Here I sit in the sun this lovely Autumn day—with tears in my eyes. Did you ever wonder why you feel blue when life is good to you? Have you pondered on why little things can seem so big? Could it be that a lot of them have piled up to a point where they seem to be overwhelming? Does it have something to do with trying to be "good" and feeling that life should be "good" to you? Do you have a preconceived notion about what life should be? Are there times when you have a chemical imbalance or when our genes take over and make life seem painful? To deal with them I could use the "People are starving in France" theory on myself (as my mom did when I didn't eat my squash). It took me a long time to figure that one out, but I finally concluded that it meant I should "count my blessings."

I could look at the person (whom I felt had wronged me) as a human being who had many good qualities and some not-so-good ones, yet was doing the best he could at the moment.

I could wallow in self-pity and say "Woe is me!"

I could get back at whomever or whatever I believed was making me feel hurt.

I could feel morally superior by playing the martyr or victim role.

Have you tried any or all of these actions? Which one helped you find peace and harmony and a feeling of joy instead of sadness?

Frankly, I've tried them all, numerous times, and found them to be completely useless in solving the concern which had somehow grown from a "molehill to a mountain." "Beauty is in the eye of the beholder," someone once said. So is pain. Have you ever compared someone who has a painful terminal illness but never complains about it with someone who lives comfortably with few obstacles in her life but moans bitterly about every little inconvenience? I don't think they are right or wrong or good or bad when they react in this manner. It's how they see their circumstances and how they judge people and happenings.

So, what can I do when the tears pop out unexpectedly? I can use the old familiar ineffective reactions or I can say, "Help me, God, to see this person or situation in another way. Help me use the love and forgiveness you've given me to find peace. Above all, help me to remember to do this immediately. Let it be an instant response and each time I practice it, let it grow as a part of me."

My Prayer

Dear God,

Let me be a channel of your unconditional love. Let it come to me and through me to all my loved ones, friends, and others who touch my life. Let me be the vessel into which you pour love, strength, and wisdom. Fill me with healing, humor and humility. Pour in patience, acceptance, understanding. and let me be the instrument of your compassion, and comfort. Pour this in a never-ending stream from you through me to all your children. Let them be surrounded by your love with Jesus on their right to listen and the Holy Spirit on their left to answer and guide. Help me to cope with all the lessons you send me. Teach me to speak with you each day, whether it's a day of conflict or peace. In doing so, help me to grow in faith.

Help me to follow the teaching of Jesus, my elder brother. Wherever there is pain, anger or need, help me to remember that there is a discouraged child of God, my sister or brother, crying out for love and forgiveness.

Help me to accept all my brothers and sisters with empathy and enthusiasm. Let me show them I have confidence in them. Keep me from blaming and judging those who may not agree with me. Encourage me to recognize my emotions, and ask for help with them and listen to your answer.

Thank you for letting me know that all I have to do is listen to your still small voice.

Amen

References

Dinkmeyer, D. and Losoncy, L.E., *The Encouragement Book,* New Jersey: Prentice-Hall, 1980.

Dreikurs, R. and Soltz, V., *Children: The Challenge,* New York: Hawthorn Books, 1964.

Gill, D., *Quest,* New York: Ballentine. Random House, 1980.

Gordon, T., *Parent Effectiveness Training,* New York: Peter H. Wyden Inc., 1970.

Halpern, H.M., *Cutting Loose,* New York: Simon and Schuster, 1977.

Halpern, H.M., *No Strings Attached,* New York: Simon and Schuster, 1979.

Hay, L., *You Can Heal Your Life,* California: Hay House, 1984.

Jampolsky, G.G., *Love is Letting Go of Fear,* New York: Bantam Books, 1979.

Progoff, I., *At A Journal Workshop,* New York: Dialogue House Library, 1975.

Shinn, F., *Game of Life,* New York: Simon and Schuster, 1986.

Siegel, B.S., *Love, Medicine & Miracles,* New York: Harper & Row, 1986.

Siegel, B.S., *Peace, Love & Healing,* New York: Harper & Row, 1989.

Simonton, C., *Getting Well Again,* New York: Bantam Books, 1988.

Small, J., *Transformers,* New York: Bantam Books, 1992.

Williamson, M., *A Return To Love,* New York: Harper Collins, 1992.